The Simp

Of

Awakening

Pointers To The Ease of Being

Based on the Meditations, Investigations, Contemplations
and Experiences
of over Forty Years of Spiritual Search and Practice
By Colin Drake

Copyright © 2015 by Colin Drake

First Edition

ISBN: 978-1-329-06716-5

All rights reserved. No part of this book shall be reproduced or transmitted, for commercial purposes, without written permission from the author.

Published by Beyond Awakening Publications, Tomewin

Cover design, photography and other titles by the author:

Beyond the Separate Self
The End of Anxiety and Mental Suffering

A Light Unto The Self
Self Discovery Through Investigation of Experience

Awakening and Beyond
Self-Recognition and its Consequences

Awareness of Awareness - The Open Way

The Happiness That Needs Nothing
Pointers to That Which is Always Here

Freedom From Anxiety and Needless Suffering

Poetry From Beyond The Separate Self

Poetry From Being A Light Unto The Self

Poetry From Awakening and Beyond

Poetry From Awareness of Awareness

Poetry From The Happiness That Needs Nothing

Humanity Our Place in the Universe
The Central Beliefs of the Worlds Religions

All of these titles are available as: e-books and in hard copy at
http://www.lulu.com/spotlight/ColinDrake

Contents

Introduction	4
Chapter Synopsis	15
Preface – Awakening is Extremely Simple	20
Prologue – Simplicity and Complexity	28
One – Two Very Simple Meditations	33
Two – Internet Discussion About Awareness	41
Three – The Ease of Being	49
Four – The Simplicity of Zen Awakening	54
Five – Internet Discussion About Awakening	60
Six – Compassion and Spirituality	67
Seven – No Higher or Lower, Sacred or Profane	74
Eight – 'Mental Illness', Awakening and 'Others'	81
Nine – Internet Discussion About Enlightenment	90
Ten – Fear of Death and Lack of 'Spiritual Achievement'	100
Eleven – Nurturing The Bliss	106
Twelve – Awakening and Suffering	115
Thirteen – The Myth of The Awakened State	125
Fourteen – Reason - Its Uses Before and After Awakening	131
Fifteen – Internet Discussion About The Absolute	142
Sixteen – Awareness - The Myth	152
Seventeen – A Creation Story	159
Eighteen – The Juice is in the Resonances	162
Nineteen – 'Levels' and 'Facets' of The Absolute	165
Twenty – Two Sides of The Same Coin	175
Twenty One – Different Strokes for Different Folks	178
Twenty Two - To Do or Not To Do-That is The Question	182
Twenty Three – Simplicities and Glimpses of 'What Is'	187
Appendix One - Investigation of Experience	191
Appendix Two - Instruments of The Absolute	201
Addendum – All or Nothing	206
The Author – A short spiritual biography	210
Glossary	216
Bibliography	218

Introduction

What follows is vital to 'new readers' whereas, those of my previous books may skip to the 'chapter synopsis' if they wish. This is not advisable unless they have realized that, at the deepest level, they are Pure Awareness – the constant conscious subjective presence. Also the first portion contains information regarding the framework within which this book was written and its objectives, which I hope would be of interest to all readers.

Introduction

The main aim of this book is to act as a stand-alone guide to, and practices for, Awakening and is mostly composed of articles, replies to questions and discussions on Awakening (in an Internet group dedicated to this) since the publication of *Freedom From Anxiety and Needless Suffering*. The thrust of the book is that the initial Awakening which reveals that, in essence, we are Pure Awareness is very simple to obtain. Then this needs to be established by repeated Awakenings due to the natural tendency to 'nod off' and re-identify oneself as a separate object in a universe of separate objects. When one is awake then anxiety and unnecessary mental suffering disappear, for these are caused by this misidentification which causes us to see each other, and the world, through a murky filter of self-interest, self-concern, self-promotion, self-aggrandizement, self-loathing, the list is almost endless. It is this world-view that causes the anxiety and mental suffering based on concern for the future and feeling we are bound by the past.

On Awakening one discovers that there truly is no separate self and so this filter is removed allowing us to see the world 'as it is' with no self-concern for the future or past. When one fully realises that there is no separate individual self then all the needless burdens of self-image, self-importance, self-promotion, self-interest, self-cherishing, self-hate, self-loathing, self-anything ... are lifted and remain so as long as one remains awake in this realisation. This gives a great ease and lightness of being which is (en)lightenment in the literal sense of the word ...

Introduction

The main theme of this (and all of my) book(s) is that of self-identity – who, or what, are we in essence? What is it that is at the core of our being, deeper than the surface level of mind/body, thoughts and sensations? To discover this is vital, for without a clear idea of one's essential identity one cannot relate to the world, and others, in an appropriate way. For, if we believe that we are separate objects, in a universe of separate objects, then we will naturally treat ourselves and others as objects, which I think we can see to be an unsatisfactory arrangement. For this tends to lead to blatant self-interest and exploitation of our fellow beings, the outcome of which is apparent in the modern world.

So the quest is to inquire and discover that which is beyond objectification, the deeper level that is the perceiver, the subjective level in which objects (thoughts and sensations) come and go.

The easiest way to find out is to investigate our moment to moment experience, which reveals that our deepest essence is Awareness, and the framework for this investigation is given in appendix one. At this stage we need to become clear as to the meaning of the term 'awareness' which has two meanings which we must not confuse. The phrase 'awareness of Awareness' utilises both of these meanings and for this reason I have used a capital letter (when using this expression) for the second one so that they may be easily distinguished in what follows[1].

Introduction

The first occurrence (awareness) is synonymous with mindfulness, that is 'seeing' with the mind, or keeping (something) in the mind. It also means 'becoming conscious of', noticing, or perceiving, as in 'I became aware of ...' This is the normal everyday usage as in the OED definition of 'aware' – *having knowledge or perception of* ...

So the term 'awareness of Awareness' means becoming conscious, or having knowledge or perception, of Awareness. We now need to define this Awareness which is simply the total 'seeing' and perceiving (or seer and perceiver) of everything detected by the mind and senses, whereas awareness (becoming aware of) is the partial 'seeing' of those thoughts/sensations on which the mind is focussed, or which are noticed. So these are not different, awareness just being a limited version (or incidence) of Awareness.

This is easy to directly experience by closing one's eyes and seeing whether you can simultaneously be 'aware of' (notice) all of the thoughts/mental images and sensations that are occurring. This is found to be impossible and yet these are all there in Awareness, which becomes apparent when one focuses one's mind on , or turns one's mind to, any of them.... and there they are! About this I wrote the following in *Beyond The Separate Self*:

---

[1] In general, throughout all of my books, whenever I use the word 'awareness' I am using this as Awareness (The Totality which is 'aware' of all) unless it is in the phrase 'awareness of Awareness' which the following discussion addresses.

Introduction

It is obvious that we would not 'know' (be aware of) our own perceptions without Awareness being present. This does not mean that we are always conscious of each one of them, as this is dictated by where we put our attention, or upon what we focus our mind. However, all sensations detected by the body are there in Awareness, and we can readily become conscious of them by turning our attention to them. It is also true that our thoughts and mental images immediately appear in Awareness, but these require less attention to be seen as they occur in the mind itself. So Awareness is like the screen on which all of our thoughts and sensations appear, and the mind becomes conscious of these by focusing on them.

Take, for example, what happens when you open your eyes and look at a beautiful view: everything seen immediately appears in Awareness, but for the mind to make anything of this it needs to focus upon certain elements of what is seen. 'There is an amazing tree', 'wow look at that eagle', 'what a stunning sky', etc. To be sure, you may just make a statement like 'what a beautiful view', but this does not in itself say much and is so self-evident as to be not worth saying!

The point is that the mind is a tool for problem-solving, information storing, retrieval and processing, and evaluating the

Introduction

data provided by our senses. It achieves this by focusing on specific sensations, thoughts or mental images that are present in Awareness, and 'processing' these. In fact we only truly see 'things as they are' when they are not seen through the filter of the mind, and this occurs when what is encountered is able to 'stop the mind'.

For instance, we have all had glimpses of this at various times in our lives, often when seeing a beautiful sunset, a waterfall or some other wonderful natural phenomenon. These may seem other-worldly or intensely vivid, until the mind kicks in with any evaluation when everything seems to return to 'normal'. In fact nature is much more vivid and alive when directly perceived, and the more we identify with the 'perceiver', as Awareness itself, the more frequently we see things 'as they are'. [2]

This Awareness is the constant conscious subjective presence in which our thoughts/mental images and sensations arise, abide, are spied and subside. Before every one of them Awareness is present, during each one of them they are 'seen' by This and This is still here after they go. Just check this out now – notice that before each thought/sensation there is Awareness of 'what is' (the totality of these at any given

---

[2] C. Drake, *Beyond The Separate Self,* 2009, Tomewin, p.14-15.

Introduction

moment) , during each of these there is Awareness of them within 'what is' and after each of them has gone there is still Awareness of 'what is'.

Rumi described this as: *the clear conscious core of your being, the same in ecstasy as in self-hating fatigue.* That is to say the Awareness in which the ecstasy or the self-hating fatigue appears. Now generally you would just be aware of, and affected by, the phenomenal state. If, however, you become aware of the Awareness in which this state is occurring and can fully identify with, and as, this Awareness then the state loses its power to affect your equanimity. For Awareness is always utterly still and silent, totally unaffected by whatever appears in it, in the same way that the sky is unaffected by the clouds that scud across it.

For more on Awareness, its correlation with nonduality and the wholeness which envelopes all manifestation see chapter sixteen.

It is this identification with Awareness that can be achieved by 'investigation of our moment to moment experience', see the appendix. When this is successfully accomplished and you can see that at the deepest level, <u>you are Awareness itself</u> then this is an Awakening. If this cultivated by remaining 'aware of Awareness' (and identified as Awareness) then this leads to full Awakening.

Introduction

At this stage it would be advisable to carry this out by following the instructions provided in the appendix. When this is successfully undertaken one becomes aware of the constant, conscious, subjective presence – Pure Awareness – that is at the centre of our being. Following from this is the realization that, as That, we are instruments through which That can sense, contemplate, experience, engage with, act in, and enjoy the physical world. This realization is dealt within the second appendix and it would be advisable to consider that now. These appendices come from previous works but are necessary inclusions so that the reader may approach this book with the requisite preparation, and also to make this work complete in itself.

Each chapter should be treated as an aid to your enquiry into the nature of Reality, and as such should not just be read and intellectually considered but need to be taken slowly, step by step, not moving onto the next step until one fully 'sees' the step that is being considered. This does not mean to say that one needs to agree with each statement, as any investigation is personal, but one needs to understand what is being said. Also to get the most out of each chapter one needs to spend some time contemplating it until one 'feels' what it is pointing to; if a chapter is just read without due attention then its significance may well be missed.

If the results of your investigations are that you discover the Pure Awareness that is at the core of your being and can identify with, and

Introduction

as, This then this is an Awakening. However, this Awakening will be readily veiled by one's previous identification with the body/mind. To overcome this one needs to:

> be committed to completely identifying with the deeper level of Pure Awareness, for in this there is always perfect peace and repose. Before this complete identification with Pure Awareness is established one will flip/flop between identifying with Awareness and identifying with a mind/body. Awakening is an ongoing process with complete identification with Pure Awareness as the final goal. For it is in fact a series of Awakenings, which is very necessary due to our natural tendency to go back to sleep! Every time we 'flop' back to identifying ourselves as mind/body we have nodded off again; and so the 'flip' to identifying with the deeper level of our being is another Awakening. The author knows this only too well, and makes no claim to 'lack of sleep'. As one investigates and cultivates this deeper level, the periods of 'wakefulness' are prolonged and consequently one 'nods off' less. The period of time between one's first Awakening and being completely awake is indeterminate and varies greatly from being to being. However, this is not a problem, for as the periods of 'wakefulness' (which are totally carefree) increase so will the commitment to identifying with the level of Pure Awareness. This will lead to more reflection and investigation, resulting in

Introduction

further Awakenings which will continue the process. To call it a process may seem a misnomer for when one is 'awake' there's no process going on, but the continual naps keep the whole thing running.

This commitment to identifying with the level of Pure Awareness involves having faith in our body/mind to negotiate living in the world, for this is what it has evolved to do. This 'complete identification' will not happen all at once but is something that has to be cultivated. I would recommend doing this by spending three periods of at least twenty minutes, every day, totally relaxing into the recognition of Pure Awareness. The best times for this are between getting up and engaging in one's daily activities, after the day's work is over and just before going to sleep. The first 'sets one up' for the day, the second refreshes and re-energises one after the day's toil, and the third aids in achieving a deep and peaceful night's sleep. One may argue that there is not enough time available for this, but these meditations provide so much relaxation and recharging that one can easily recover the time by sleeping for an hour less.[3]

So Awakening is not for the dilettante, the dabbler, but is a full-time proposition as is pointed out in the addendum 'All or Nothing'.

---

[3] C.Drake, *Beyond The Separate Self*, 2009, Tomewin, p.89-90

Introduction

One other thing that should be noted is that this book is mostly composed of individual articles and discussions which have been published on the internet. They are given as pointers and aids for the reader's own investigations into, and contemplations on, the problem of self-identity. There is necessarily some duplication between them as what is being discussed is so simple. They are different 'takes' on the same simplicity, presenting the material in various ways whilst building upon what has been discovered, so some repetition is unavoidable. It should also be noted that each of these are, as far as is possible, stand-alone meditations or contemplations, thus needing to make sense by themselves. Therefore some sections of each will contain similar passages, so that they are relatively complete when read in isolation.

If you have any comments, questions or feedback you are welcome to contact me at colin108@dodo.com.au

Introduction

Chapter Synopsis

The preface is a short analysis and poems which highlight the simplicity of Awakening to the fact that at the deepest level one is Pure Awareness – The Constant Conscious Subjective Presence. This should not be read until one has successfully completed 'Investigation of Experience', given in appendix one, and can 'see' (at least intellectually) the deeper level of Pure Awareness that is the substratum of our being.

The prologue discusses the absolute simplicity of this method of Awakening and compares this with the many complex systems, ideologies and categories of (mis) identification which seem to appeal to the human mind.

Chapter one contains two meditations which result in identifying with, and as, Pure Awareness. The first is my own which I developed after my first Awakening in 1996, based loosely on 'self-inquiry'. The second is on that I stumbled upon in 2005 when I Googled 'Pure Awareness', and is from the Dzogchen school of Tibetan Buddhism. I was amazed at the similarities between them as I had never been exposed to Dzogchen, or any form of Tibetan Buddhism, when I formulated mine.

Introduction

Chapter two is a discussion on the subject of Awareness in which the questioner was unable to 'see' it and I was attempting to clarify the whole subject.

Chapter three highlights some of the outcomes of Awakening which lead to experiencing the true 'ease of being' free from existential angst and self-concern.

Chapter four shows the simplicity of Awakening as espoused by two famous Zen masters.

Chapter five is a discussion on Awakening and whether it is immediate, or gradual, and whether repeated 'Awakenings' are required.

Chapter six considers the question of compassion and the apparently uncompassionate actions/responses by seemingly 'spiritual' individuals.

Chapter seven posits that, as everything is a manifestation of Consciousness, then the categories of 'sacred or profane' and 'higher or lower' are meaningless, and that their use causes separation.

Chapter eight is an email discussion with a reader suffering from a diagnosed mental illness who has not let that negate his Awakening.

Introduction

This also touches on whether there are other 'points of Consciousness' in humanity, or whether there is only the one Consciousness.

Chapter nine contains a very informative discussion between many people on the question, and definition, of Enlightenment.

Chapter ten considers the fear of death and the tendency to be attracted to other spiritual paths due to seeming lack of progress

Chapter eleven is a practice for feeling, and then nurturing, the bliss of using the body as an instrument of Consciousness through which that can feel Its own manifestation – the physical world.

Chapter twelve is devoted to a general discussion considering how Awakening relieves the suffering of the one who 'awakens' and can be used to alleviate the suffering of 'others' and the world.

Chapter thirteen debunks the myth that when one is 'awake' then one becomes a 'stone buddha' showing no seemingly negative emotions.

Chapter fourteen discusses whether after Awakening one loses the use of reason and whether this is useful in the Awakening process.

Chapter fifteen considers the question of writing about The Absolute and also Its essential nature.

Introduction

Chapter sixteen debunks the myth that Awareness is only concerned with one 'thing' noticing, or becoming aware, of another. Whereas, this is only a very limited form of the Awareness that underlies the whole of Reality.

Chapter seventeen gives a scenario for creation (among many) based on the realizations that we are Pure Awareness, in essence, and that our body/minds are instruments through which That (Consciousness) can experience and enjoy Its own manifestation.

Chapter eighteen discusses how, when examining other 'paths' or 'ways of knowing' one needs to keep an open mind so that new discoveries may occur.

Chapter nineteen is a discussion on 'levels' (not my word) and 'facets' of The Absolute, hosted on an internet group, by one who is not impressed with giving It the name Awareness.

Chapter twenty considers the equal validity of different approaches, or paths to, and names of The Absolute.

Chapter twenty one compares two different approaches to Awakening and shows how they lead to the same result.

Introduction

Chapter twenty two is a discussion that addresses the view, of many modern nondualists, that there is nothing we can 'do' to awaken or to stay awake.

Chapter twenty three is an exchange that took place on an internet group regarding the 'simplicities' that well up from within as one awakens, and how that changes the way that one views the world

Preface – Awakening is Extremely Simple

Discusses Awakening from the dream of being a separate object in a universe of such, plus poems which highlights the simplicity of Awakening to the fact that at the deepest level one is Pure Awareness – The Constant Conscious Subjective Presence.

Awakening is Extremely Simple

Awakening is simply a matter of rousing ourselves from the dream that we are separate objects (mind/bodies) in a universe of separate objects. This is achieved by inquiring into our own nature and discovering the deeper level in which thoughts/sensations occur, are seen and dissolve. This rising, existing and subsiding of thoughts and sensations is an ongoing process and that which constitutes our moment-to-moment experience. The body is experienced as a stream of sensations whilst the mind is experienced as a stream of thoughts (which includes mental images), which leaves the question of who, or what, is the experiencer??

We tend to think of this as the mind but this is obviously not the deepest level of experiencing, as the mind itself (the flow of thoughts) is just an experience! Similarly with the body where sensations occur and are detected by the nervous system, and other sense organs, this too is just an experience … We are aware of all of these thoughts and sensations and this Awareness is constant whereas the latter are ever changing ephemeral objects. Thus This is that which we feel we have always 'been' and that which seems to have been the constant unchanging basis of our lives, which has 'seen' everything we have ever experienced. So at the deepest level we are Awareness itself in which mind/body (thoughts and sensations) appears, exists, is seen and disappears on a moment-to-moment basis.

To check out whether this Awareness is omnipresent ask yourself the question 'am I aware of a time (or place) where this Awareness was not present?' By definition this can never be answered in the positive as if Awareness was not present you would not be aware of it! Even when you are in deep sleep and the mind is not active (thus not 'aware') this question cannot be answered in the positive… For in this state the question cannot be asked and there is no experience occurring, also when dreaming there is Awareness of the dreams. Therefore, in your own direct experience Awareness is omnipresent.

To verify this please investigate the following and see whether it is true in each moment:

Before each thought/sensation occurs Awareness is a constant 'background' presence. This is pointed to by the fact that there is immediate Awareness of the thought/sensation when it occurs. Just check this out …

During each thought/sensation Awareness is a constant 'background' presence and that by which it is 'seen'.

After each thought/sensation has finished Awareness is still a constant 'background' presence.

Awakening is Extremely Simple

Therefore in our own experience every 'thing' (which we 'know' by our sensation of, or thought about, it) arise, abides, is spied and subsides in this constant conscious background presence which is Awareness itself.

This is the never-changing which has been present since we were born (and before …) in which the ever-changing flow of our lives has occurred, and which has witnessed this.

Awakening

To awaken, rouse yourself from the dream,
Of being a separate object on the earth.
No matter how bewitching this may seem,
An illusion the ego has fostered since your birth

To see this, into your own nature enquire,
To discover the underlying strata,
Where thoughts and feelings rise, then expire.
The perceiver of this ephemeral data.

Awakening is Extremely Simple

The body is experienced as a flow of sensations,
The mind as a flow of images and thought.
What is it, then, that notices these presentations?
The constant subject that need never be sought.

That which we feel we have always been,
The unchanging basis of this very life,
That which all of our moments has seen,
Our ups and downs, joys, struggles and strife.

The clue is that, to live, aware we must be
Of mind and body that seem to ebb and flow;
So Awareness, itself, is That which these see.
The changeless that doesn't come and go.

Check it out in this moment, now
Notice how thoughts and sensations to and fro,
In ever present Awareness, that is how
Our experiences we can enjoy and know.

So This is what we are, have always been.
Wake up to this fact, by truly knowing
That, which our whole life-story has seen.
A constant witnessing presence, no thing!

Awakening is Extremely Simple

Awakening to Awareness is extremely simple,
More elementary than noticing a dimple …
For this is That by which 'we' know,
Our thoughts and feelings as they flow.

So, for these to feel or see,
Awareness must forever be,
Right here at the centre of our being,
That through which our eyes are seeing.

No journey to undertake,
For This cannot us forsake.
No matter how much we duck and weave,
This Ground of Being we cannot leave.

If you imagine you are apart,
One day you'll wake up with a start,
To That which you always are,
Closer than close, never afar.

In which all things come and go,
So there is no 'above or below',
No separate heaven or hell,

Awakening is Extremely Simple

As they are both in This as well.

For if Awareness could ever go missing,
You wouldn't even know when you were kissing!
Thoughts and sensations would not be 'seen',
You'd be unaware that they had been.

There's no way you could even be alive!
Happily It does not need to arrive,
As It can never ever depart,
For really truly 'That Thou Art' …

Pure, Pristine, Radiant Awareness

Pure Awareness,
Consciousness at rest,
Within Which nothing less,
Than all appears to manifest.

Radiant Awareness,
Consciousness at rest,
By Which absolutely nothing less,
Than all is seen which manifests.

Awakening is Extremely Simple

Pristine Awareness,
Consciousness at rest,
Into Which absolutely nothing less,
Than all returns to the Unmanifest.

Prologue – Simplicity and Complexity

Discusses the absolute simplicity of this method of Awakening and compares this with the many complex systems, ideologies and categories of (mis) identification which seem to appeal to the human mind.

.

Simplicity and Complexity

We have already discovered the absolute simplicity of Awakening by becoming aware of Awareness and then identifying with this, the deeper level of being in which all thoughts, mental images and sensations are seen (see appendix). Moreover, this is consciousness at rest in which all things (forms of cosmic energy, consciousness in motion) arise, abide and finally subside. However, this absolute simplicity does not appeal to the human mind which loves complexity, categorization, compartmentalization, labeling and conceptualization.

This is especially so in the area of identification, that is in defining what we actually are, and also in spirituality in general. There are various categories that are used in this process that can be seen to include most forms of misidentification – labeling us as being separate objects (in a universe of the same) or as members of an elite group, many of which claim to have comparatively deeper understanding of the truth of reality. Some of these categories are:

> **The 'Ism(s)'** – *Unspecified system, philosophy or ideological movement (OED).*
> Examples being: Buddhism, Hinduism, Islamism, Judaism, Vashnavism, Saivism etc …
> There are also more worldly examples e.g. communism, masochism, sadism, pacifism etc...

Simplicity and Complexity

The Olog(ies) – *A subject of study or interest (OED).*
Examples being: Numerology, astrology, psychology, scientology, phrenology etc…

These are considered by their devotees to be more than just interests but to actually help in defining what one is, one's actual identity.

There are again more worldly examples such as morphology, radiology, chronology etc …

The Ian(s) - *Suffixes which form adjectives or nouns (OED)* normally used in labeling.

Examples being: Christian, Australian, Siberian, Canadian, Austrian, Indonesian, etc …

A simpler version of this is 'an' e.g. American, German, Mexican etc …

Note that these also purport to say something about what we actually are. It is interesting to note that these form the noun by adding the indefinite article 'an' to the end, which implies a separate object.

The It(ies) - *Suffixes which form nouns denoting quality or condition (OED)*

Such as: Christianity, Divinity, Spirituality, Catholicity, Nationality, Personality etc …

Simplicity and Complexity

Needless to say there are many more worldly examples, but the ones given above tend to denote categories that we are associated with and say something about our identity. They even form the noun by adding 'it' which itself denotes a separate object!

This is not to say that some members of these categories do not have pointers to our true identity embedded within them, especially the religions, but they have overlaid this with so much dogma and complication that it is very difficult to unearth. So I would advise any one of you that has directly discovered that one is, at the deepest level, Pure Awareness to treat them all with kid gloves.

Especially dangerous are the tendencies to feel that one belongs to any category, as this can lead to a subtle (or not so subtle) form of tribalism, and any description of oneself that the 'system' imposes which defines one as a separate individual object. Rumi was aware of the danger of this as Coleman Barks points out:

> And he made it clear that someone who considers nation or religion an important human category is in danger from severing the heart from its ability to act compassionately. This is a radical idea now, but Rumi held this conviction in the thirteenth century with such deep gentleness that its truth was recognized.[4]

---

[4] Barks C. *The Essential* Rumi, 1995, London, P.246

For the problem is that if you identify as belonging to any particular group you will tend to favor other members of this group and discriminate against those who are non-members. Also if you identify as a separate individual object you will identify others as that and thus be liable to treat them as objects. Whereas true compassion stems from 'seeing all as oneself', that is identifying all as being of the same essence and thus essentially the same as oneself.

In fact it is best to steer clear of them all by avoiding any labeling of oneself in any way that could lead to this erroneous conclusion. The continued investigation of, relaxation into and identification with Pure Awareness is the key to achieve this. This is the simplest way to discover the true nature of self-identity without having to fight through the morass of complexity imposed by the various systems categorized above. It also conforms to Ockham's Razor given colloquially as 'the simplest solution is the best' and defined in the OED as 'the scientific principle that in explaining a thing no more assumptions should be made than are necessary'.

For, in the investigation of one's moment to moment experience (see appendix) which reveals that at the deepest level one is Pure Awareness, no assumptions need to be made or relied upon. And this also provides the simplest explanation of self-identity requiring no beliefs, just that which is directly discovered ...

One – Two Very Simple Meditations

This chapter contains two meditations which result in identifying with, and as, Pure Awareness. The first is my own which I developed after my first Awakening in 1996, based loosely on 'self-inquiry'. The second is on that I stumbled upon in 2005 when I Googled 'Pure Awareness', and is from the Dzogchen school of Tibetan Buddhism. I was amazed at the similarities between them as I had never been exposed to Dzogchen, or any form of Tibetan Buddhism, when I formulated mine.

Two Very Simple Meditations

I would like to discuss two modern, popular and powerful approaches to investigation of the Absolute Reality based on *Advaita* and Tibetan Buddhism which evolved completely independently and yet have striking similarities. The first of these is a simple meditation practice based on 'self-enquiry' a technique championed by the *Advaitist* sage Ramana Maharshi (1879-1950). The basic approach is to sit quietly and using the inquiry 'Who am I?' discover that which is deeper than body or mind, the source of all existence. When perfected the 'Who am I?' inquiry reveals that there is no separate individual self but only something that can be described as 'pure radiant Awareness'. This is defined by Sankara in the 'Vivekachudamani' as the 'self-effulgent witness of all' about which Ramana said 'effortless, choiceless Awareness is your real state.'[5] Here is the meditation practice, revealed to a follower of this school (me), stemming directly from self-inquiry:

> *If you sit quietly you can easily notice that:*
> *There is effortless Awareness of every thought.*
> *There is effortless Awareness of every sound.*
> *There is effortless Awareness of every sight.*
> *There is effortless Awareness of every taste.*
> *There is effortless Awareness of every smell.*
> *There is effortless Awareness of every feeling.*
> *There is effortless Awareness of every touch.*

---

[5] S.R. Maharshi, 'Words of Grace', 1969, Tiruvannamalai, p.18

Two Very Simple Meditations

This Awareness encompasses every mind/body experience, for they appear in it.

Deeper than thoughts (mind) and sensory experiences (body) <u>you are this Awareness</u>.

This Awareness is effortless and choiceless as it requires no effort and it is choicelessly present.

This Awareness is omnipresent. If you investigate you will find that it is (and has been) always present wherever you are. Even during sleep there is Awareness of dreams, and of the quality of that sleep.

This Awareness is absolutely still as it is aware of the slightest movement of body/mind.

This Awareness is utterly silent as it is aware of the smallest sound, the slightest thought.

This Awareness is absolutely radiant for it illuminates everything that appears in it.

Every mind/body experience arises in this Awareness, exists in this Awareness and subsides back into this Awareness.

Two Very Simple Meditations

At the deepest level you are this pure, radiant, still, silent, boundless, changeless Awareness.

As this Awareness there is nothing to achieve, for how can you achieve what you already are?

As this Awareness there is nothing to find, for how can you find what you cannot lose?

As this Awareness there is nothing to desire, long for or get, for how can you get what you already have?[6]

The second is another very simple meditation practice from the Dzogchen school of Tibetan Buddhism. Sogyal Rinpoche, the author of 'The Tibetan Book of Living and Dying is from this lineage and he has been teaching, in the West, since 1974. About meditation he said: 'The purpose of meditation is to awaken in us the sky-like nature of mind, and to introduce us to that which we really are, our unchanging Pure Awareness, which underlies the whole of life and death.'[7] Here is the practice, from a follower of this school, that was posted on the internet:

---

[6] C. Drake, 'Beyond the Separate Self', 2009, Halifax, p.29
[7] S. Rinpoche, 'The Tibetan Book of Living and Dying', 1992, San Francisco, p.59

Two Very Simple Meditations

Dzogchen Awareness practice

Get comfortable and let mind and body really relax - no need to sit in any strict meditation position - relaxed in a comfy chair is fine.

Locate Awareness in space and then put attention on the breath flowing in and out quite naturally.

After a few minutes, cease to focus on any particular object and practice 'choiceless Awareness', simply observing whatever objects arise and pass in Awareness. Notice the following about each object:

  It is impermanent

  It has no existence apart from Awareness, Itself.

  Being a form of Awareness, it is transparent to it.

1. Without fixing attention on anything, just consider:
Is there Awareness of sights? Is there Awareness of sounds? Is there Awareness of sensations? Is there Awareness of thoughts? Is there Awareness of feelings? Tastes? Etc. This very Awareness which is right here now, IS that eternal, self luminous Reality that you have been striving to realize all along. Since this Awareness is already here, your striving is unnecessary.

2. Abandon all concepts about experience and simply observe. See how appearances arise in Awareness. Since whatever

Two Very Simple Meditations

appears is already present, how can it be avoided?
See how appearances pass in Awareness. Since whatever has passed is no longer present, how can it be grasped?
See how everything appears in Awareness without the least obstruction.
Since nothing obstructs appearances, there are no obstacles to be removed.
See how everything passes in Awareness without the least hindrance.
Since everything is self-liberating, there is nothing to be set free. Relax into this effortless contemplation of how things actually are.

3. Without making any adjustments, continue to observe: Although you say, 'forms arise in Awareness,' can you really separate
Awareness from its forms? Is not Awareness like an ocean and forms its waves?
Because Awareness and forms are ultimately inseparable, duality never existed. How then can it be transcended?
Although you say, 'I am aware of such and such object,' can you truly distinguish between yourself and the object? Where does 'self' end and 'object' begin?
Because subject and object are, in reality, indistinguishable, delusion never originated. How then can it be dispelled?

4. Look! Reality is staring you in the face:
You say you cannot eliminate your 'self' but there is no self to eliminate.
You say you have not attained 'Enlightenment' but there is not the slightest thing to attain.
You say, 'I am ignorant of my true identity' but how can this be? What else is there besides this infinite, eternal, non dual field of Awareness-and-form which is already present, right here and
now....and now...and now.....

Therefore, surrender all desire for attainment and just be what you are, Awareness, Itself![8]

So comparing the two we can see that they both agree that our natural effortless Awareness of thoughts and sensations is 'that eternal self-luminous reality' in which forms arise, exist and subside, and that in essence we are that Awareness. They both agree that there is nothing to attain, i.e. all striving is unnecessary; also that there is nothing to desire, grasp or get. There is also agreement that this effortless Awareness is here and now. So all that ultimately exists is this 'Pure, radiant, omnipresent field, of effortless choiceless Awareness' in which everything arises, appears to exist, and subsides without ever any

---

[8] www.geocities.com/sphurna/awareness

separation or duality. Thus here we have two 'schools' one of which posits *Atman* (The Self) and the other *Anatta* (no self) arriving at almost exactly the same conclusion without any collusion.

Two – Internet Discussion About Awareness

A discussion on the subject of Awareness in which the questioner was unable to 'see' it and I was attempting to clarify the whole subject.

Internet Discussion About Awareness

AS posted this discussion topic:

Who knows the sensation of the thirst or the sensation of a hot pan on the skin? Logically, we can conclude that it is Awareness - because logically we can argue that one needs to be aware in order to know anything. However, that is just a logical deduction and not a real experience.

At the time of the experience, there is no real separate Awareness apart from what is actually experienced. The logical conclusion of separateness and the thought of "I am aware (or, I am Awareness) and I know of the thirst, touch or pain" only arises in the thinking, only as a logical deduction.

Experience and Awareness arise together. True, there is no experience without Awareness. But, there is also no Awareness without experience. When you think have Awareness without experience - that itself is yet another experience.

• Me: From the intro to 'Awareness of Awareness - The Open Way':

The easiest way to find out is to investigate our moment to moment experience, which reveals that our deepest essence is Awareness itself, and the framework for this investigation is given in appendix one. At this stage we need to become clear as to the meaning of the term 'awareness' which has two meanings which we must not confuse. The phrase 'awareness of Awareness' utilises both of these meanings and for this reason I have used a capital letter (when using this expression) for the second one so that they may be easily distinguished in what follows.

The first occurrence (awareness) is synonymous with mindfulness, that is 'seeing' with the mind, or keeping (something) in the mind. It also means 'becoming conscious of', noticing, or perceiving, as in 'I became aware of ...' This is the normal everyday usage as in the OED definition of 'aware' – having knowledge or perception of ...

So the term 'awareness of Awareness' means becoming conscious, or having knowledge or perception, of Awareness. We now need to define this Awareness which is simply the total 'seeing' and perceiving (or seer and perceiver) of everything detected by the mind and senses, whereas Awareness (becoming aware of) is the partial 'seeing' of those thoughts/sensations on which the mind is focussed, or which are noticed. So these are not different, Awareness just being a limited version (or incidence) of Awareness.

This is easy to directly experience by closing one's eyes and seeing whether you can simultaneously be 'aware of' (notice) all of the thoughts/mental images and sensations that are occurring. This is found to be impossible and yet these are all there in Awareness, which becomes apparent when one focuses one's mind on, or turns one's mind to, any of them.... and there they are!

Internet Discussion About Awareness

- AS: At the time of no "external" experience... ...IT can feel like Light/Awareness/Radiance/Presence...
The question then is... ...what if that itself is yet... ...another experience?
After all, this experience too changes... ...sometimes it just feels like spaciousness...

- Me: If it 'feels' like anything then it is indeed another experience.

- AS: You can say Awareness has no attributes - but, then, "how" you know it?

- Me: You can know that it is present by the simple fact that when a thought or sensation occurs there is Awareness of it i.e. you are aware of it.

- AS: That makes sense as a logical conclusion. However, that is not a real, direct experience. Light and Awareness have an amazing parallel. Light can't be seen unless it hits and reflects from an object. The Awareness is not seen unless it illuminates an object.

- JE: Awareness without consciousness. Try going into samadhi just as you are about to fall into sleep. If you are lucky, you will enter the state of Awareness without consciousness. In deep sleep, there will be

Internet Discussion About Awareness

Awareness but no consciousness, nothing else, no 'me' story. When you wake up that Awareness will slowly recede in the background as consciousness, the world and your 'me story' floods in.

Don't ask me how I remember that I was aware during deep sleep. Perhaps it gets somehow recorded in the physical brain memory.

And this Awareness without consciousness has been talked about by many gurus.

• Me: In response to AS's last. That is exactly the point Awareness is present because it does 'illuminate' our thoughts and sensations ... that's why it is called 'radiant'. Without it they would not be 'seen' by the mind!

Also by definition Awareness is always pure for all things arise, abide and subside in this leaving it unaffected, thus no thing 'taints' it. In your own experience this can be easily noticed, how thoughts, images, and sensations come and go in Awareness leaving it unaffected. This is the meaning of 'pure' - untainted or unaffected - this does not imply that it is without content, just that this content has no effect on It. In fact one cannot become 'aware of Awareness' when there is no content, for the content is what makes Its existence apparent. In the same way that if you were to look at an infinite lake, reflecting the sky, you would not see it if it were absolutely still but if a stone were thrown into it then the ripples (the content) would make it visible.

- AS: Colin: it does make logical sense to conclude that Awareness might be present even without an experience. But, by the very definition... ...the "Awareness without experience"... can not be directly known or experienced, it can be only logically concluded.

- Me: Awareness saturates the whole of manifestation, from electrons changing their behaviour when (aware of) being observed (see the double-slit experiment), cells responding to (aware of) changing environments, white corpuscles attacking viruses they detect (are aware of) in the blood, moulds moving towards (when aware of) foods placed near them and so on ...

- Me: At all events I am glad that you were aware of my comments for us to have this discussion and of my photos to enjoy them.

- AS: Colin:, you bring another interesting point about the Awareness. Each cell of our body has numerous electrons. According to what you said above, the electrons can be said to be aware... ...yet, I am not aware of the electrons, their Awareness or of what they do. Nor am I aware of the cells, their Awareness or their actions. Nor am I aware of

Internet Discussion About Awareness

the white corpuscles, their Awareness or of what they do. What kind of Awareness then I am? It seems to me that my scope is quite limited.

- AS: Colin:, of course! Thanks for being here! I hope I don't annoy you too much

- Me: Not at all, I am glad of the opportunity to 'crack a tough nut' as they say, even if I do not succeed!

Now back to your previous point, when you say you 'I am not aware' you mean that your mind cannot see ... this is the small instance of Awareness, mentioned in my long opening statement. Please reread this very carefully to see whether you can see the difference between this and (the overall) Awareness in which all occurs.

And indeed, as you say, your (humans) scope is very limited. When you consider that there are an infinite range of wavelengths available and our eyes/ears can only detect a very small range of these ... Also our other senses only detect a very limited 'range' of possible 'sensations' ...

Here is a post by AS a few weeks later:

Internet Discussion About Awareness

The body is human. You are NOT. You are Awareness.

Basic Nonduality or Advaita is very simple. It is the knowledge that you are NOT your thoughts, ideas, opinions or body. You are not what you sense, feel, know or perceive. You are the Awareness. Just as in your dream, dream characters and experience rise and fall in you and you, the Awareness remain unchanged; so, it is Right Now, You, the Awareness, remain unchanged and untouched by the experiences, feelings and thoughts that rise and fall inside you.

When you pay attention to the Awareness, you are, you experience clarity and freedom. When you pay attention to the thoughts, you experience denseness and constrictions. It is like paying attention to the SKY versus the clouds. Like clouds floating in the Sky, thoughts float in Awareness. Rather than focusing on fixing the "clouds" (thought), one might simply shift the FOCUS to the Sky (Awareness), that one Truly IS and experience the Clarity that is never lost.

To which my reply was: Alleluia!

Three – The Ease of Being

Highlights some of the outcomes of Awakening which lead to experiencing the true 'ease of being' free from existential angst and self-concern.

The Ease of Being

On Awakening one discovers that there truly is no separate self and so this filter is removed allowing us to see the world 'as it is' with no self-concern for the future or past. When one fully realises that there is no separate individual self then all the needless burdens of self-image, self-importance, self-promotion, self-interest, self-cherishing, self-hate, self-loathing, self-anything ... are lifted and remain so as long as one remains awake in this realisation. This gives a great ease and lightness of being which is (en)lightenment in the literal sense of the word ...

When one identifies with Awareness each moment is encountered freshly and directly, uncoloured by past experiences. Most of our mental suffering and frustration is caused by our mind judging our experience as unsatisfactory, or by projecting into the future and worrying about the imaginary problems that this might hold. Whereas from the viewpoint of Awareness itself each moment is enough (in itself) as Awareness does not judge but just witnesses 'what is'. With this outlook one is much more capable of handling what the world may throw at us, as each moment is taken as it comes without relating it to the past, future or any imaginary self-image based on identifying with thoughts and sensations (mind/body). This does not imply that life will be without problems just that we will become more able to solve these as they arise.

With regard to solving these problems we have at our disposal the most amazing instrument, the human mind, our own inbuilt onboard computer. This is a wonderful problem solving device, but to function properly it needs to be supplied with accurate data. All computer errors are due to incorrect data or program bugs. The main program bug in the mind occurs when we identify ourselves as the mind. In this case it colours all of the data it receives with its own opinions, judgements, self-interests and so on, which naturally leads to erroneous conclusions. As we learn to identify with the deeper level of Pure Awareness, this bug is fixed, and we learn to see things 'as they are', rather than through the filter of the mind. Now data is fed in uncontaminated, and problem-solving activity continues more accurately and spontaneously.

So when one is 'awake' each moment is encountered freshly and responded to (rather than reacted to) appropriately, which enhances our problem-solving ability, thus making life easier and more enjoyable. There are also many other by-products of Awakening which enhance the 'ease of being', which each have a chapter devoted to them in my other books, some examples of which are given below:

This leads to being completely 'At Home' in the universe, free from existential anxiety and angst, utterly at peace (for Pure Awareness is Consciousness at rest, still and silent), absolutely free to be what one is, feeling completely accepted and loved in 'the place where you flourish and from which you originate (OED)'.[9]

---

[9] C. Drake, *Home is Where the Heart Is,* in **Beyond The Separate Self,** 2009 Tomewin p.63-65

Which also leads one to being 'Simply Free to Be', free from (that is unconstrained by) beliefs, ambitions, desires, conditioning etc... with no shoulds and should nots, cans and cannots, past and future, totally here now in this moment.[10]

One also discovers that no thing 'matters'[11] or has any existential meaning. From this it follows that no 'thing' can affect what you are, in essence, and that all labels which have been assigned to you are essentially meaningless.[12]

This identification also takes one beyond karma as Awareness is totally unaffected by anything that is occurring within it. That is to say that although old thought patterns continue to come up one will no longer be compelled, or constrained, by them. They will just appear as 'clouds' scudding across the 'sky' of Awareness leaving it totally untroubled, for in this case one does not identify with them or take them as indicators of who, or what, one is. In the same way experiences which could be attributed to one's karma, good or bad, lose their power to affect one's essential underlying equanimity.[13]

---

[10] C. Drake, *Simply Free to Be,* in **Beyond The Separate Self***,* 2009 Tomewin p.27-39
[11] C. Drake, *Nothing Matters,* in **Beyond The Separate Self***,* 2009 Tomewin p.66-70
[12] C. Drake, *Nothing has Essential Meaning,* in **A Light Unto Your Self***,* 2011 Tomewin p.150-158
[13] C. Drake, *Awakening, Karma and Renunciation,* in **Awakening and Beyond***,* 2012, Tomewin p.87-95

The Ease of Being

One also discovers 'The Fundamental Secret' (as opposed to 'The Secret') which is that 'each moment is enough' as Awareness just witnesses 'what is' at any given moment without needing to change it or wishing for it to be different. This realization can be a 'magic bullet' which can be applied to overcome boredom, envy, greed, insomnia and many other mind created (non existent) problems. Then one can replace the (Secret's) mantra of 'ask, believe and receive' with 'investigate, realize and relax'![14]

When one identifies with Awareness, and lives as That, one can abandon all externally imposed ethical frameworks (although it's probably more comfortable to abide by the local laws!) confident in the knowledge that Pure Awareness needs no guidelines to act for the best. Then one can, in the words of Khalil Gibran, let one's 'song-bird' freely fly ... That is acting spontaneously and responding to situations rather than reacting to them.[15]

---

[14] C. Drake, *The Fundamental Secret,* in ***A Light Unto Your Self***, 2011 Tomewin p.89-95

[15] C. Drake, *Awakening and Ethics,* in ***Awareness of Awareness***, 2013 Tomewin p.116-120

Four – The Simplicity of Zen Awakening

This chapter shows the simplicity of Awakening as espoused by two famous Zen masters.

The Simplicity of Zen Awakening

Below are two expositions by Zen masters, with commentary, which show the utter simplicity of Awakening. In the first it is realizing 'one's true heart', that is one's fundamental essence, Pure Awareness, and pledging oneself to this. In the second it is to recognize the spiritual light (of Pure Awareness) manifesting through the six senses that has never been interrupted. That is to see that the detections of the senses appear in, and are seen by, Pure Awareness.

Bukko, a great Zen master, said[16]:

> The way out of life and death is not some special technique; the essential thing is to see through to its root.
> *That is to say That in which life and death appear.*
> This is not something that fell from heaven or sprang up from the earth.
> *It is not external to oneself, but is the deepest level of our very existence.*
> It is at the centre of the functioning of every man, living with his life, (not) dying with his death, becoming a Buddha, making patriarch. These are all in dependence on it, and one who goes into Zen has to pierce and break through to this thing.
> *Actually It is not a 'thing' but That which perceives all 'things', the constant conscious subjective presence, Pure Awareness, Consciousness at rest. It is also That on which all depends,*

---

[16] Osho, *The Language of Existence,* 1988, Cologne, p.48-49

being the essence of all existence. At the physical level Awareness saturates the whole universe and no living organism could survive without it.

What is called Zen sitting is not some sort of operation to be performed, and to take it so is wrong. In our line, it is simply realizing what one's own true heart really is, and it is necessary to pledge oneself to the true heart.
One's own true heart is this Pure Awareness ('Big Mind' in Zen), the heart of the (and all) matter, what one truly 'is', and the essence of Zen is to realize this. Then one needs to full commit (pledge oneself) to this realization by staying awake and reAwakening (by this realization) every time one 'nods off'.

Going into Zen is seeing one's original nature, and the main thing is to make out what one was before even father or mother were born. For this one must concentrate one's feeling and purify it, then, eliminating all that weighs on one's thought and feeling one must grasp the self.
Consciousness, at rest as Pure Awareness, and in motion as cosmic energy – the manifestation - is the essence of all and That which we were before any human came into existence. The realization of this, and identifying with and as This, is to grasp the self. The outcome of which is that thoughts and feelings are

seen for what they are, fleeting objects, and so they lose their 'weight'.

We are saying that the self seeks to grasp the self, but in fact it is already the self, so why should it go to grasp the self? *Because we misidentify ourselves with the fleeting objects (thoughts, feelings, sensation and mental images) rather than the constant subject presence, that is as the perceived rather than the perceiver. In this we are identified as a separate object (or collection of these) in a universe of such.*

It is because in the mass of knowings and perceivings and judgements, the true self is always so wrapped up in the distinctions and exclusivities that it does not emerge to show itself as it is.
It is not the true self that is wrapped up in these, but the mind, and as most of us identify with our minds we do not see 'it' (ourselves) as it is (we are).

Rinzai, one of the most famous of all Zen masters, said[17]:

In all the varieties of our daily activities is there anything lacking? The spiritual light manifesting through the six senses

---

[17] Osho, *The Language of Existence,* 1988, Cologne, p.72-73

has never been interrupted. He who is able to perceive it in this manner can be an unconcerned man for the rest of his life.

This spiritual light is the radiance of Awareness, for it is by this that all things are 'seen' and by which the detections of the senses are perceived. Awareness is Consciousness at rest which has never been interrupted, the constant conscious subjective presence that is the deepest level of our being. Manifestation, cosmic energy, is also Consciousness but in motion and therefore of the same essence. Identification with This, that is seeing that we are expressions (and instruments) of This removes all self-concern; which is caused by misidentification with an illusory abiding 'self' – as a separate object in a universe of such.

There is no peace in the three worlds which are like a house on fire.

It is not a place for a long stay for the murderous demon of impermanence will, in an instant, make no choice between the noble and the humble, and the old and the young.

This misidentification can only cause suffering as it makes one feel that one is an object in the three worlds which will eventually perish due to its impermanent nature.

If you do not wish to differ from the patriarch and the Buddha, it will suffice for you to seek nothing outside.

The Simplicity of Zen Awakening

Once the realization (that one's deepest level is Pure Awareness and that the body/mind is a fleeting expression of This) has taken place, then no external seeking is necessary.

If, in the time of a thought, your pure and clean no-mind shines, this is your own Dharmakaya buddha [Rigpa or 'Big Mind' - Aware Nothingness]
If, in the time of a thought, your passionless no-mind shines, this is your own Sambhogakaya buddha [The Radiance of Rigpa or 'Big Mind']
If, in the time of a thought, your non differentiating no-mind shines, this is your own Nirmanakaya buddha. [The Manifestation of Rigpa or 'Big Mind']
The no-mind shines when one is identified with the radiant Awareness that is at the core of one's being.

This threefold body is the one who is now listening to my expounding of the dharma. This can only be achieved if nothing is sought from without.
This realization comes from directly investigating one's own nature, see the appendix, and not from external seeking. Once the realization has been made then one can truly 'call off the search'.

Five – Internet Discussion About Awakening

A discussion on Awakening and whether it is immediate, or gradual, and whether repeated 'Awakenings' are required.

Internet Discussion About Awakening

GJ: via Conscious Variety

What is spiritual Awakening? Is it a matter of a moment or is it a matter of a lifetime?

Spiritual Awakening in Slow Motion

Awakening, in this context, is the sudden loosening of our belief in thoughts as being in any way definitive of the inner self. The thinking mind, in a way, breaks open, through its own circulation, absurdity or conflict, and the consciousness that supports the...
consciousvariety.com

Me: One awakens in a moment but this is only full Awakening if one does not 'nod off' again. After the first Awakening this is likely due to force of habit as one has been asleep for so long. This then requires another Awakening and so on until one no longer nods off...

• DL: This is going to sound like I'm being clever, but I don't mean it that way. I mean it very sincerely. The main "symptom" of Awakening that I notice in my life, is that I now have no interest in Awakening. In one way it seems absurd to call myself awake--the only way I might say that is by comparing it with some memory I have of being "in a different state" than I am now. That seems a ridiculous and pointless exercise. At the same time, for most of my life, I've been in a state of anticipating some resolution to my subtle seeking energy. Something began to shift, over a period of about two weeks, as I remember it, and since that time, that seeking project, and all of its energetic logic, is just gone--I can't find it anywhere. That seeking person seems irrelevant to me now. Anything besides breathing the fullness of this moment, which feels to extend infinitely in every direction, seems irrelevant. There's nothing to compare it to.

- Me: I agree but this is not the common case. Most of my correspondence is with those who have had an Awakening but continue to suffer by nodding off ...

- SA: Awakening is a story. Some stories can take a moment, some stories can take a lifetime. Awakening to the story is timeless.

- Me: Giving up the story of who we think we 'are' is essential to, and some would say synonymous with , Awakening . Re-identifying with the story is nodding off again .

- DL: Yes, I haven't seemed to have the "nodding off" thing. Not yet, anyway. It's been about two years--I could be having a kind of "honeymoon" experience. As Sam says, it's a story--and one I'm not

Internet Discussion About Awakening

that interested in, personally, although in another way I am fascinated to understand it in an "academic" way, because I seem to have a teaching dharma of some kind, and there's a motivation to refine my language, to be able to communicate with others in a useful way.

- GJ: It has always seemed to me that the phenomena of nodding off - why, what, how, is part of the miracle. Something to do with integration and the channelling of consciousness through different layers of form.

- DL: What I relate to, in terms of "nodding off," would be the very long "anticipatory" period I had prior to the "Awakening" I mentioned (which I really think of as a "grounding in" more than an Awakening-- like what used to be a kind of "from the neck up".

Relative to "grounding in" vs. "waking up," there is the idea around, that there are two basic modes of Awakening, i.e., "top down" vs. "bottom up." I seem clearly to be a "top downer," but we seem to be very much in the minority. I don't actually run across much that addresses the top down phenomenon. I'd greatly appreciate whatever people have to share in this regard.

- EI: It's to get out of the shower and realizing you left your towel in your bedroom which happens to be at the other end of the corridor. Namaste

- Me: For most people nodding off always eventually produces some kind of unnecessary mental suffering. This is where 'vigilance' comes in for this can be used as a wake up call that one has nodded off. ReAwakening can then be as easy as seeing that one is aware of this suffering and that one is this Awareness (the constant conscious subjective presence) and not the suffering which is just an ephemeral object appearing in This.

At this point a comment was made about this being 'shallow Awakening', starting with 'For The Love of God!' and then ranting on people having 'shallow Awakenings' and not being of any value because the person (aware presence) has not seen the emptiness of all concepts. Upon my following rebuttals this comment was deleted!

- Me: To get deep into the ocean you have to walk through the shallows, and many keep returning to the shore due to their conditioning. Luckily 'the love of god', as you put it, will spur them on to deeper Awakening.

Another point is that the 'wetness' of bathing in the shallows is the same 'wetness' as bathing in the depths. In the same way 'shallow Awakening' , if there is such a thing, is the same as 'deep Awakening' and can only occur because the person (aware presence) has seen the

Internet Discussion About Awakening

emptiness of all concepts. It's just that their previous conditioning (samskaras) takes over and masks this 'seeing'.

- DL: Colin: Is it your feeling that this nodding off can largely be prevented, or at least mitigated, by the appropriate use of something like inquiry? IOW, does it seem to you to be greatly a kind of psychological backsliding into conditioned mental patterns, more so than a deeper energetic phenomenon?

It does seem natural that conditioned patterns would re-assert themselves to some degree, for a time, after an initial Awakening. If the Awakening is profound, there won't be the sustaining soil in place to support them very much, however. I'd think they would leave of their own accord, in relatively short order. I'm sure a good teacher or sangha can help with this, also.

Me: Yes I do recommend repeated inquiry using a framework which I developed where you directly investigate your momentary experience, and this reveals that you are, in essence, Pure Awareness. These are my comments from 'Beyond The Separate Self':

One needs to be totally committed to completely identifying with this deeper level of Pure Awareness, for in this there is always perfect peace and repose. Before this complete identification with Pure Awareness is established one will flip/flop between identifying with Awareness and identifying with a mind/body. Awakening is an ongoing process with complete identification with Pure Awareness as the final goal. For it is in fact a series of Awakenings, which is very necessary due to our natural tendency to go back to sleep! Every time we 'flop' back to identifying ourselves as mind/body we have nodded off again; and so the 'flip' to identifying with the deeper level of our being is another Awakening. The author knows this only too well, and makes no claim to 'lack of sleep'. As one investigates and cultivates this deeper level, the periods of 'wakefulness' are prolonged and consequently one 'nods off' less. The period of time between one's first Awakening and being completely awake is indeterminate and varies greatly from being to being. However, this is not a problem, for as the periods of 'wakefulness' (which are totally carefree) increase so will the commitment to identifying with the level of Pure Awareness. This will lead to more reflection and investigation, resulting in further Awakenings which will continue the process. To call it a process may seem a misnomer for when one is 'awake' there's no process going on, but the continual naps keep the whole thing running.

Six – Compassion and Spirituality

Considers the question of compassion and the apparently uncompassionate actions/responses by seemingly 'spiritual' individuals.

Compassion and Spirituality

Today there were three topics on the internet that made me wonder about the lack of compassion that can occur in various 'spiritual' outlooks.

Firstly, I got a post from a Satyananda group about 'universal love' in which it suggested that this comes about when one nurtures humility and obedience to the guru, thus diminishing the personal ego. However, the recent revelations regarding Swami Satyananda and his exploitation of his female devotees made me realize the dangers of this path, especially if one is in a sexually vulnerable position. When one reads the posts on this page it truly makes one wonder how such a seemingly exalted being could show such callousness and lack of compassion.

For me (and many of his students) this is all the more poignant as I spent many years following him and learnt many wonderful yogic techniques (such as asanas, kirtan, yoga-nidra, meditation and kriyas) from him, the first three of which I still use regularly. My only response to this can be to follow Sri Ramakrishna's advice which is - if the teachings of a guru enhance one's spiritual life then use them, even if the guru's character is questionable. For these practices have enhanced my life immeasurably and my daily hatha yoga session and lunchtime yoga-nidra are invaluable, whilst the monthly kirtan (that we hold here) is the high point of each month.

Compassion and Spirituality

So all I can conclude is that learning techniques from a guru can be very useful but one needs to be very discriminating when it comes to 'surrendering' to any other (potentially flawed) human being.

Secondly, I had this exchange with XX who had posted a paragraph on an internet group devoted to nonduality, which contained the following:

> "When you recognize that all thoughts are made up ... you will no longer suffer because taking things personally will only make you laugh."

This evoked the following exchange:

- Me: You can only not take 'things' personally when you realise that there is no separate self ...

XX: Since it is all made up it is ALL funny.

Me: Once again, it's only funny whilst one is not misidentified as a separate object in a universe of such...

XX: Oh Colin, it's funny that way too, trust yourself, it's all funny. Using Diunital Consciousness there is a separate self and no separate self occupying the same space at the same time. That's the beauty of

Oneness (non-duality) it includes both and everything as itself. And if that don't make you chuckle... I'm not right or left in the head.

Me: It might be funny for you, and it sure is for me, but it's not funny for those who don't realize oneness ... just look around you!

XX: Everywhere I look it simply makes me laugh. Me, you them, others, us it all tickles my funny bone. Even the seriousness is funny from here.

Thirdly, here is another post on the same group in the wake of a particularly bad terrorist attack:

> Another Non-Dualist responds to the Paris Shootings. His response: "Shootings are Fun".

All of which made me somewhat perplexed as to how such 'spiritual beings' could seemingly show such lack of empathy and compassion for the suffering of others. This is especially the case for anyone purporting to be a Non-Dualist, for in nondual Awakening all are seen to be of the same essence (Pure Consciousness) as oneself. Thus the suffering of 'others' is also the suffering of oneself. Now it is true that most mental suffering is self-imposed by misidentification (of oneself as a separate object in a universe of such) and thus one cannot truly take this seriously. Although, there is still compassion for the suffering that this appears to cause, which is obviated by the Awakening of the 'sufferer' caused by correctly identifying oneself as an expression, and instrument, of Consciousness. So the best way to reduce the amount of this suffering in the world is to point as many people to Awakening as possible.

Another way to reduce suffering is to create as much joy, for oneself and 'others' as one can. As I wrote in 'Why Do Anything' (in *Awakening and Beyond)*:

> As the purpose of creation is for the enjoyment of the Absolute (Consciousness), and we are all instruments (and manifestations) of This, then it stands to reason that we should create as much joy in our lives as possible. Moreover, when we find a way to enable others to enjoy their lives more this is as valuable, in fact more valuable if we can facilitate this for a group, as creating joy for ourselves. This is the ethos of Utilitarianism, a secular philosophy first espoused in the 18th century, whose creed is: 'when making a decision, that involves other people, one should always adopt the position that creates the greatest amount of happiness for the largest number of people, whilst regarding one's own happiness as being no more important than that of anyone else'. Bearing all this in mind, it

becomes apparent why humans are naturally compassionate and become more so as they align themselves with the purpose of creation by Awakening. So this gives the reason for the ultimate question you have asked, which is: 'why would I want to do anything?' For the pure joy of living and to create as much joy in the world as possible!

The best way to achieve both of these aims is to help others awaken, for this not only reduces their suffering but also often gives them much joy in the form of blissful experiences. This not only makes them happier but it also produces much joy in the one who is 'pointing' to Awakening. As the Dalai Lama said 'I believe the purpose of life is to be happy', which he qualified by saying:

> From my own limited experience I have found that the greatest degree of inner tranquility comes from the development of love and compassion. The more we care for the happiness of others, the greater our own sense of well-being becomes... It is the ultimate source of success in life. [18]

I know in my own case that when I receive emails from my readers detailing their Awakening and the joy that this has produced it really 'makes my day'. So you can see that aiding others, in 'going beyond the separate self' and realizing that they are expressions and

---

[18] C. Drake, *Humanity, Our Place in The Universe,* 2010, Tomewin, p.71

instruments of Consciousness, is a win-win situation for those who are 'pointers' and those who awaken.

With regard to suffering that is caused by external circumstances that are beyond one's control, we can at least empathize with those affected, donate to groups that help these if we are able, and aid anyone that we meet that is in this category.

Seven – No Higher or Lower, Sacred or Profane

Posits that, as everything is a manifestation of Consciousness, then the categories of 'sacred or profane' and 'higher or lower' are meaningless, and that their use causes separation.

No Higher or Lower, Sacred or Profane

Since becoming semi-retired, as the demand for hand-made pottery has declined and I have become eligible for the old-age pension (thank you Australia!), I have taken up reading novels and listening to talking books. Presently I am listening to *Master and Commander*, by Patrick O'Brian and reading *The Night Manager*, by John le Carre ... both of which are very entertaining. On discussing this with a friend they said that they didn't read fiction but only read 'higher' books, which made me think that this might be necessary for them until they came to the realization that there is no 'higher' or 'lower'! It also put in mind the concept, promoted by Western Religions (of 'The Book'), of 'sacred' and 'profane'.

For both concepts are dualistic, dividing the world into opposing categories and overlooking the essential Oneness, Consciousness, that is at the heart of all being (and non-being!). To show that all apparent 'things' are manifestations of the same essence consider the following from 'Nonduality' in *A Light Unto Your Self*:

> This can be shown by investigating the nature of our own subjective experiences, which is actually all that any of us have to investigate. For each of us any external object or thing is experienced as a combination of thought (including mental images) and sensation, i.e. you may see it, touch it, know what it is called, and so on ... Thus everything in the external world is experienced as a mixture of thoughts and sensations, and

when we attempt to investigate any 'thing' it is these that we are investigating.

In any given moment of direct experience there are only three elements: thoughts (including all mental images), sensations (everything detected by the senses) and Awareness of these thoughts and sensations. All thoughts and sensations are ephemeral objects (the perceived) which appear in this Awareness (the perceiver) which is the constant subject. So at a deeper level than the ever-changing objects (thoughts and sensations) we are this constant subject, Awareness itself.

To put this in a slightly different way, we can easily notice that every thought and sensation occurs in Awareness, exists in Awareness and dissolves back into Awareness. Before any particular thought or sensation there is effortless Awareness of 'what is': the sum of all thoughts and sensations occurring at any given instant. During the thought or sensation in question there is effortless Awareness of it within 'what is'. Then when it has gone there is still effortless Awareness of 'what is'.

Reiterating, for each of us any external object (or thing) is experienced as a combination of thought and sensation, i.e. you see it, touch (feel) it, know what it is called, etc. Therefore in our direct experience everything arises in, exists in and subsides back into Awareness itself.

Awareness can also be defined as universal Consciousness when it is totally at rest, completely still; aware of every movement that is occurring within it. In our direct experience we can see that Awareness is still, as there is Awareness of the slightest movement of mind or body. In fact this is the 'stillness' relative to which any movement can be known. Every 'thing' that is occurring in Consciousness is a manifestation of cosmic energy, for the string theory[19] and the earlier theory of relativity show that matter is in fact energy, which is Consciousness in motion (or motion in Consciousness). For energy is synonymous with motion and Consciousness is the substratum, or deepest level, of all existence.

Now all motion arises in stillness, exists in stillness, is known by its comparison with stillness, and eventually subsides back into stillness. For example, if you walk across a room, before you start there is stillness, as you walk the room is still and you know you are moving relative to this stillness, and when you stop once again there is stillness. In the same way every 'thing' (Consciousness in motion) arises in Awareness (Consciousness at rest), exists in Awareness, is known in Awareness and

---

[19] This posits that all 'things' are composed of 'strings' of energy in complex configurations, vibrating at various frequencies.

subsides back into Awareness. Awareness is still, but is the container of all potential energy which is continually bubbling up into manifestation (physical energy) and then subsiding back into stillness.

Thus there is no dichotomy or duality between the physical world and 'Awareness' for they are both manifestations of the same essence. The physical universe is just cosmic energy (Consciousness in motion) when it is manifest into physical form, and Awareness (Consciousness at rest) contains this same energy in latent form as potential energy. Therefore there is in reality no multiplicity (nonduality) as there is only Consciousness existing in two modes, in motion and at rest.

Once this is truly 'known' by deeply identifying with, and as, Pure Awareness (see appendix one) then this can lead to being 'in love' with the whole of creation which entails seeing nothing as 'higher' than anything else and also seeing everything as being 'holy' – that is as a manifestation of the Absolute Reality, The Divine, Consciousness itself. Even if this 'loving' does not occur the realization of 'Oneness' overcomes the dualistic outlook which imposes the labels of 'higher', 'lower' 'sacred' or 'profane'. Also, the realization that life forms are instruments through which That can experience, and enjoy, Its own manifestation (see appendix two) gives validity to all forms of harmless enjoyable entertainment whatever 'others' may think. About this I wrote in *Awakening and Beyond*:

> If yielding to the temptation in question does not harm oneself, or another, or lead to misidentification, then by all means yield; otherwise just watch it from Pure Awareness without following it, identifying with it, or buying into it and it will just fade. Enjoy life to the full I say! For this I find that 'moderation in all things' is the key, as pleasures wane if over-indulged in and are at their best when tasted sparingly ... in the same way the tastiest fruits tend to be the small ones. As far as rules, moral codes, commandments etc. are concerned - a pox on them all!! Let's just scrap them all and replace them with: 'do what you want as long as you do not hurt others'. If you wish to hurt yourself that's your business, but for Awakening it would be more advisable to stick to the first statement.

The key, as with most correct understanding, is to come to a valid conclusion regarding self-identity – who (or what) are we in essence. For, without this our world-view will be, at best, confused and more than likely heavily coloured by looking through the filter of self-interest, self-concern, self-aggrandizement, self-image, selfishness etc. The realization that we are in essence Pure Awareness leads to seeing that there is no small self, obliterating this filter and allowing us to see the world clearly and 'as it is' undefiled by spurious opinions and preferences. Moreover, 'higher' and 'lower', 'sacred' and 'profane' are themselves products of these and not objective labels. Thus, when these are seen to be of no weight then such labels also lose their meaning.

Eight – 'Mental Illness', Awakening and 'Others'

An email discussion with a reader suffering from a diagnosed mental illness who has not let that negate his Awakening. This also touches on whether there are other 'points of Consciousness' in humanity, or whether there is only the one Consciousness.

'Mental Illness', Awakening and 'Others'

Here is an email exchange I had regarding whether there are 'points' of consciousness in 'other people, or whether there is only the One Consciousness. It also highlights the fact that 'mental illness' need not stop one from Awakening and can actually help in the process!

Dear Colin

Thank you so much for this [a mailed out article], which has come at just the right time! :) I was diagnosed recently with borderline personality disorder, and am currently attending a therapy group. I have struggled for years with mood swings and other symptoms. What has become clear, through inquiry, is that Awareness does *not* experience mood swings: that it openly embraces, loves, everything. So there are still difficult periods; but unless thought is bought into, nothing is "wrong" as such.

I do have one question, although as I write it, I can see that it is very much a mind-based query! It's a bit of an old chestnut, too. It has to do with "other people": through inquiry, it has become more and more clear that there is only ever this consciousness; and within it, thoughts, sensations and perceptions -- some of which are labelled "me", some of which are labelled "other people". But it is all appearing here, in the one Knowing. So does this mean there really aren't other "points" of consciousness in "other people"? That it is all just arisings in this

'Mental Illness', Awakening and 'Others'

consciousness? For if we say that there is more than one consciousness -- then would it still be One? But couldn't this be solipsism? I was at work the other day, and got hit by a wave of loneliness -- there are no others! Just this Awareness! But at other times, this feels like the sweetest, warmest intimacy -- all, everyone, is closer than close.

Hope that makes sense! Thank you again.

Love, XXXX

Dear XXXX, Good to hear that although you are undergoing therapy for mood swings you have clearly realised that these are only mental phenomena and that Awareness (your essence) is unaffected by these. So by this potent 'seeing' you know that there is indeed 'nothing wrong' and that when you are identified with this Awareness you openly embrace, and love, everything. This is indeed the sweetest warmest intimacy as you say.

The labelling of 'me' and 'others' only applies to the surface level of body/mind and these physical expressions are indeed unique different manifestations[20], and instruments, of the One Consciousness. Thus they will have different psychological make-ups but behind all of these is the same Pure Awareness[21], aware of all the varying experiences that

---

[20] Consciousness in motion, cosmic energy.
[21] Consciousness at rest.

they have. So although there is only the One there are as many 'streams of consciousness' (thought flows) as there are minds, but these all arise in, abide in and subside back into Pure Awareness.

Your term 'points of consciousness' is misleading for there is only Consciousness. This has been likened to an ocean of which 'we are' only drops, but these drops are of the same essence as, and constitute, the ocean. As 'spray' (apparent separate manifestation) they may appear to have different shapes and sizes but on falling back into the ocean these vanish and they merge with it again, losing any seeming individuality that they had.

Loneliness is 'sadness because one has no friends or company' (according to the OED) and could naturally occur if your ephemeral manifestation (body/mind) has no affectionate interaction with other body/minds. But as this clearly shows this is only problematic (producing sadness) if one is identified with the body/mind, for at the deepest level there is indeed the sweetest warmest intimacy of (the One) Awareness.

That is not to say that there is not a great deal of comfort in the company of like-minded 'souls' (now there's a mis-used word!) and such 'Satsang' is indeed recommended for we all need support in our commitment to Awakening*. So if you encounter any I would recommend that you nurture their company, alternatively you could

'Mental Illness', Awakening and 'Others'

look for groups in your area that point to, and nurture, this*. I know, from my own experience, that these are difficult to find, for many that appear to do this are very dogmatic in their approach and this is often counterproductive and thus not conducive to Awakening, or remaining awake.

In fact, although I do have some good friends that are very helpful in this endeavour, I regard the group with whom I share my emails as my Sangha and receive much 'nourishment' from my interactions with them. As I'm sure you know, I share these as often as I feel to be reasonable and many others are also 'nourished' by them. So, although we may not physically meet we are joined by cyberspace and thus able to encourage each (seeming) other.

Once again I am pleased to hear of your realization that there is 'Just This Awareness!' and would encourage you to hold to That! Love, Colin

Here is his response with my response imbedded in italics:

Dear Colin

Thank you from the heart for your clear and generous response: your words really helped clarify the matter. Having mental illness has been a strange experience: in the mind-story, I have suffered really since late adolescence, but it fully developed in my twenties. There has been a lot of struggle, lots of counselling, trips to doctors, psychiatrists. I still certainly have bad days.

It's wonderful to hear that with all of the above you still recognize the fact that you are Pure Awareness and are nourished by this.

The mind has found different grooves into which it tries to fit experience: sometimes positive stories (as if mental illness is a mark of being "special"); sometimes (more often) negative ("I must have done something bad in a past life ..... this is bad karma ......why am I not more spiritual? ...."). But this is all the stuff of thought, isn't it?

Yes, that's all it is and means absolutely nothing about who you are!

Without referencing concepts, there is just experience happening; life dancing its myriad dance. I have also found that mental illness has been a strange kind of gift, as it forces one to look clearly at what is happening: it exposes the mechanism of suffering, and is a reminder of how the mind-made self is not as powerful or "in control" as it likes to think! It tends to bring one to one's knees.

That's great, for it has lessened the power of the mind, by your clear seeing, and has prepared you for the final act of (small) self-surrender.

'Mental Illness', Awakening and 'Others'

I completely agree about sanghas: I am a member of different groups on internet; but to be honest, I sometimes avoid them, as they are often beset with people arguing out the finer points of Buddhist teachings, or emptiness vs. Awareness, essentialism vs non-essentialism etc. (different views on karma, reincarnation, and so on). This kind of thing just seems to fire up anxious thinking in me ("I haven't got it! This stuff about karma scares me!"), and I can feel the small self contracting, concretising.

Once you are awake you are beyond karma in that Awareness itself is totally unaffected by anything occurring in it and thus when complete identification with Awareness takes place karma is powerless! That is to say that although these old thought patterns continue to come up one will no longer be compelled, or constrained, by them. They will just appear as 'clouds' scudding across the 'sky' of Awareness leaving it totally untroubled, for in this case one does not identify with them or take them as indicators of who, or what, one is. In the same way experiences which could be attributed to one's karma, good or bad, lose their power to affect one's underlying equanimity.

Sometimes I honestly don't think the differences between schools matter so much: what matters is what is in the heart; is everyday kindness, happiness, non-judgementalism. It's got to come back to Love, in this moment, and then this moment. Just noticing its pervasive all-presence, being it.

Well said, I completely agree … it all comes back to love, that is no-separation where all is this presence.

Take care, my friend, and thank you deeply again!

Love, XXXX

I echo the last two lines.

Here is a follow up email relating another perspective on 'mental illness'

> This is a really fascinating article -- not really non-duality, but a shamanic perspective on "mental illness":
>
> http://www.jaysongaddis.com/2010/11/the-shamanic-view-of-mental-illness/
>
> Love XXXX

And my reply:

'Mental Illness', Awakening and 'Others'

> Dear XXXX, Thanks for that, it's very interesting and something I had long suspected ... that many so-called 'mental illnesses' were spiritual emergences, or that their symptoms were manifestations of other states of consciousness which were not recognized by western doctors/psychologists etc. I will use this link in future articles. Love, Colin

If any of you have an interest in the link between 'mental illness' and Awakening, or 'spiritual emergence' I would strongly advise you to check out the website given above.

Nine – Internet Discussion About Enlightenment

A very informative discussion between many people on the question, and definition, of Enlightenment.

AS

.... What is Enlightenment in your opinion? ....

I have read many definitions of enlightenment:

1. Enlightenment = end of mental suffering. End of anger, lust, passion, jealousy, greed, fear, complains, hate, shame, guilt and all other kind of mental pain and suffering.

2. Realization = knowledge that I am consciousness right now. I am not the body nor am I my thoughts nor I am a person, nor I am the changing mind. I am the witness of it all. I am the space in which it all arise and fall. It is simple knowledge and it has nothing to do with any particular experience. Experiences come and go, that is their nature.

3. Enlightenment = end of I. End of the belief in the separate, independent, isolated durational existence.

4. Enlightenment = end of the belief in free will. End of the belief in control over results.

5. Enlightenment = end of separation. Belief in the separate I is the belief in the separation. Belief in the independent separate self is the belief in separation. Belief in the person is the belief in separation. Belief in soul is the belief in separation.

Internet Discussion About Enlightenment

6. Realization = Peace.

7. Enlightenment = end of seeking = end of wanting something other than the reality of the moment

8. Enlightenment = full acceptance of the present moment

9. Enlightenment = end of the belief in the self existence

10. Enlightenment = complete self acceptance

11. Enlightenment = complete self love

12. Enlightenment = complete surrender

13. Enlightenment = end of thinking

14. Enlightenment = complete mental rest

15. Enlightenment = knowing that the grass grows, the wind blows and I don't do any of it

16. Enlightenment = knowing that the thoughts pass through me, I am not the thinker of the thoughts.

17. Enlightenment = end of attachment

18. Enlightenment = Knowing that experiences pass through me. I am not the experiencer.

19. Enlightenment = end of attachment to experiencing

20. Enlightenment = letting of the urge to control and judge

21. Enlightenment = end of thinking oneself as an entity in time and space

22. Enlightenment = knowledge that the time and space are INSIDE me. I am NOT inside time and space.

23. Enlightenment = end of time and space

24. Enlightenment = knowledge that the Universe is INSIDE me. I am NOT inside the Universe.

25. Enlightenment = knowledge that the Universe and I is ultimately one

26. Enlightenment = deep dreamless sleep

- WK: I would say it's just seeing directly rather than seeing through thought.

Out of your list I liked number 7 most though.

- NT: Nice collection. Many of them are equivalent but highlight different (practical) facets

- MC: My favourite definition is "SHUT UP!"

- CH: Enlightenment is simply "what is." It's your "Ordinary mind."

- KO: Enlightenment is a word, a meaningless sound until and unless we attach a meaning to it.

- ML: Those who seek the light are merely covering their eyes. The light is in them now. Enlightenment is but a recognition, not a change at all. Light is not of the world, yet you who bear the light in you are alien here as well. The light came with you from our native home, and stayed with you because it is your own. It is the only thing you bring with you from Him Who is your Source. It shines in you because it lights your home, and leads you back to where it came from and you are at home. This light can not be lost.

- PM: entering the light meant to be

- ER: Realizing that we have no control.

Internet Discussion About Enlightenment

- FM: Reminds me of the Zen story of the Zen master who sat in a cave for years. Some towns people were walking by his cave and suddenly saw the cave light up and a brilliant flash of light emanating from within. The Zen Master walked out with peace and tranquillity on his face. The towns people asked, "What have you attained?" ZM says, "I have overcome anger." The towns people said, "oh, that's amazing." Then someone spoke up, "Anything else, oh great ZM?" Zen Master says, "No, All forms of anger do not affect me." A few minutes pass and someone else spoke, "but surely you've reached another level of enlightenment or something." Zen Master screams, "Look you damn idiot fools are you deaf? No, just the release of anger!! Geesh.." and he storms back into the cave. Enlightenment lasts until it doesn't. I guess??

I have no idea why I wrote this out. but here it is...???

- PS: I know why you wrote that. So I can tell you that anger can be broken, and like a tamed wild bull be driven into the market place without upsetting apple carts. But, sometimes, apple carts need to be overturned and apples need to be spilled.

- EC: After years of practice and study, I can tell you that what I though enlightenment was when I began was a bunch of nonsense.

- PS: You are right, enlightenment is a deep peace beyond the senses.

- Me: When one fully realises that there is no separate individual self then all the needless burdens of self-image, self-importance, self-promotion, self-interest, self-cherishing, self-hate, self-loathing, self-anything ... are lifted and remain so as long as one remains awake in this realisation. This gives a great ease and lightness of being which is (en)lightenment in the literal sense of the word ...

- TG: If "God-realization" is simple non-suffering (which is neutral, really), the human race is screwed beyond all recognition... maybe nature made a mistake. It's like "the end of my pain is ultimate bliss?" Are we in hell?
I was discussing this with my brother last night.. if all the good things in life are simply relief from sufferings, maybe to stay alive is idiotic and to die is wise... why the hell would you hit yourself over the head with a hammer to get the pleasure of stopping?

- Me: When suffering is removed the natural, innate, bliss of being bubbles up. This is my, and many others, direct experience .

- TG: I've "tried" simply being without taking an interest in one's surroundings, and it's painful... it's like "duh, duh, duh, duh" repetition that seems to go on and on. So I do not agree, because my experience differs.. I wonder if maybe life is innately suffering, so we have to seek reliefs from it. Time has to be filled, we have to be distracted from the endless ticking of the clock.

- Me: When one stops seeing things through the filter of the small self they appear much more vivid and alive .... once again my, and many others, direct experience

- TG: ah. Well, I'm not sure how one can talk about anything that isn't past (indirect) experience, but if u say so...

- Me: My present experience is that my surroundings are full of interest ... vivid and alive.

- TG: Okey doke... well, enjoy, if you're out there...

- Me: Thank you, it would be nice if you were out here too ...

- Me: In fact that's the only reason I write, in an attempt to point ways of going 'Beyond The Separate Self' ... to enable others, by their own investigations, to see the world (and all 'others') in this way too. That is as an expression, and manifestation, of (and in) the Consciousness that underlies the seeming physical 'reality'.

- MC: Enlightenment = a mythical state of transcendence.

- TG: Maybe transcendence is just clarity or understanding... but quite honestly it doesn't result in bliss or happiness, only freedom from confusion. Ignorance is bliss, not clarity.

- Me: In your experience ...

- KB: Clarity is not like cotton candy, but it almost always feels better than ignorance.

- TG: Well Colin, "ignorance is bliss," "the truth hurts" and "disillusionment" as a not-good-feeling thing are concepts known and used as early as kindergarten, so I don't believe "my experience" is something far-out or uncommon, for what it's worth.

Me: I never said it was, it is just your experience. We can all only rely on our own experience and what is discovered by investigating that ... on this subject I have uploaded a framework for this investigation into 'files'. It is called, naturally 'investigation of experience' which you might like to check out some time.

This is given in appendix one, about which Ramaji , an American spiritual teacher and author of many books, said:

it is a step by step method for doing that which, if you do it diligently, will inevitably lead you to the true foundation of your moment to moment experience as well as the universe itself. For those of you who cannot read between the lines, I just said it will take you to "enlightenment."

This is (en)lightenment in the literal sense of the word ... for it takes you beyond the (illusory) separate self to identifying with (and as) Pure Awareness. As long as this identification is maintained the ease and lightness of being will remain.

Ten – Fear of Death and Lack of 'Spiritual Achievement'

Considers fear of death and the tendency to be attracted to other spiritual paths due to seeming lack of progress.

Fear of Death and Lack of 'Spiritual' Achievement

Here is an email exchange between myself and a purchaser of my latest, *Freedom From Anxiety and Needless Suffering,* concerning fear of death and the tendency to be attracted to other paths. My comments are imbedded in his email in italics.

Dear Colin

Thank you so much for your recent emails, and your wonderful latest book, which I have downloaded -- so clear and beautiful! Lovely reviews by Ramaji, too. Sorry I haven't written more lately -- have been very busy with teaching (and marking!).

Interesting times here -- I find myself drifting 'in and out' of peaceful recognition: there are periods where I feel very clear, and then others where thoughts and problems become mesmerising again. There are often particular kinds of thoughts which feel especially compelling: I find myself worrying about what will happen after death, for example, or feeling that I am spiritually 'unworthy', or brooding on the past.

Who is this I? It is the clinging to a particular stream of Consciousness within the ocean that causes any anxiety. This attachment to a particular stream of Awareness[22] also brings up questions about karma

---

[22] That is Consciousness at rest, in which all manifestation, cosmic energy – Consciousness in motion (or motion in Consciousness) arises, abides and subsides.

Fear of Death and Lack of 'Spiritual' Achievement

and reincarnation, both of which can only apply to a particular object (or set of them). When one is not identified as such but just as an expression (and instrument) of Consciousness itself then these are irrelevant. For as I say in 'Awakening and Beyond':

> *Awareness itself is totally unaffected by anything occurring in it and thus when complete identification with Awareness takes place karma is powerless! That is to say that although these old thought patterns continue to come up one will no longer be compelled, or constrained, by them. They will just appear as 'clouds' scudding across the 'sky' of Awareness leaving it totally untroubled, for in this case one does not identify with them or take them as indicators of who, or what, one is. In the same way experiences which could be attributed to one's karma, good or bad, lose their power to affect one's underlying equanimity.*[23]

Some traditions believe that we are reincarnated until correct identification occurs, about this Ramakrishna said:

> *As long as a man remains ignorant, that is to say as long as he has not realized God, so long will he be born. But after attaining knowledge he will not have to come back to this earth, or any other plane of existence.*[24]

---

[23] From *Awakening, Karma and Renunciation* in *Awakening and Beyond*

[24] The Gospel of Ramakrishna, tr by Sw. Nikhilananda,1942, Ramakrishna-Vivekananda Centre, New York p.416

Fear of Death and Lack of 'Spiritual' Achievement

Whereas, Nisargadatta said that he did not believe in reincarnation[25]. But ultimately the question is irrelevant once correct identification has taken place for then both opinions amount to the same thing. The (Mahayana) Buddhists also believe that one can choose to be reincarnated after one has awakened to help others to awaken, but even if this were to be the case this should not cause any angst as after Awakening all mental anxiety ceases.

Thus Awakening and realizing that 'The Kingdom of God is within you' (Luke 17 v.21) overcomes all worry and angst allowing us to fully engage with the world as expressions (and instruments) of Consciousness (God) without fear of, or concern for, the future. This takes us beyond the reaches of karma and makes irrelevant all questions of what happens after the dissolution of the physical body ...[26]

I guess the key is to keep inquiring, and to remain with the clarity that no thought is ultimately true -- however much it might seem to assert itself!

That's right, just the discovery that, at the deepest level, you are the Pure Awareness in which these fleeting thoughts come and go ...

---

[25] R.Powell, *The Ultimate Medicine of Sri Nisargadatta,* 1994, Delhi, p.199
[26] From *The Kingdom of God* in *The Happiness That Needs Nothing*

Fear of Death and Lack of 'Spiritual' Achievement

Another kind of thought that seems to rear its head is that of 'more': I begin to look at various teachings, with different emphases -- and the thought comes -- 'Maybe I should be doing that... or that... and making more progress... and deepening...' Or: 'Am I enlightened?' I guess this is all part of thought's smoke-and-mirrors routine: it seems to be defending its life, its storylines! It will endlessly proliferate problems if it can, generating doubt, uncertainty, fear.

With regard to this see the attached[27], there's always more power, achievements, status that can be had to bolster the ego. Even the thought that 'I am enlightened' is misidentification for it posits a separate 'I' that can achieve something. You seem to have sussed it all out in your 'guess' ... a good one!! Also there's no need to achieve anything once you have awakened (and I can assure you that you have ... many times!) for, when awake, 'each moment is enough' in itself, see attached.[28]

Thank you again, my friend; I find your inquiries and meditations so useful (and also the 'short moments of Awareness' practice). I hope you are keeping well.

I am glad that you find the practices useful. It's always best to stick to one path once you have discovered the one that suits you best, for

---

[27] *Simplicity and Complexity* from *Awareness of Awareness – The Open Way*
[28] *The Fundamental Secret* from *A Light Unto Your Self*

dabbling in others is liable to cause confusion. I myself do investigate other paths but only to look for the harmonies between them and my own ... not to try out their practices or achieve their goals. As far as keeping well is concerned, That (Pure Awareness) which we all are is always exceedingly well!! Once identified with That then wellness is one's natural state even if the body is not always in that condition ... But thank you for your kind wishes, Love, Colin

Love XXX

To finish this article here is his reply:

Thanks so much for this, Colin!

have you seen this beautiful clip? It really shows Awareness loving the simplicity of experience -- almost a mini, 40-second satsang!

https://www.youtube.com/watch?v=5X-sTpWJlAg

Love XXXX

Eleven – Nurturing The Bliss

A practice for feeling, and then nurturing, the bliss of using the body as an instrument of Consciousness through which that can feel Its own manifestation – the physical world.

In a recent article 'Love Loving Itself' I described a method for experiencing the Absolute (Pure Awareness – Consciousness at rest – the deepest level of our being - the lover) loving the beloved (the manifestation – Consciousness in motion) using the physical body as its instrument for this. I have recently discovered that if one lengthens this practice, concentrating on the subtle bliss of embodiment then the mind becomes still and the bliss slowly increases …

If you like light some subtle incense to add to the atmosphere in the room and brush your teeth (or eat something pleasant) to ensure that there is an agreeable taste in the mouth. Make sure that the phone is on silent and that the 'do not disturb' sign is on the door.

Lie, or sit, in the <u>most comfortable position you can possibly find</u>, with your eyes closed. I would recommend Shavasana (the corpse pose) lying flat on your back with your legs slightly apart, feet falling gently outwards, and your arms slightly away from the body with your palms facing upwards. Do this on a bed, couch, or soft carpet with a cushion or pillow under the head. If you are cold or hot then adjust your clothing/covering until your temperature is perfect. If you are in pain then take a pain killer an hour before this practice, or if in great pain then, if possible, vary your pain management strategy until no pain is present. The point is to adjust your circumstances, if possible, to the point where there is absolutely no discomfort.

So now lying in absolute comfort, notice that Awareness is always present and that it is very easy to see that for this to be the case there is absolutely nothing the mind needs to do. Similarly there is no problem that the mind needs to solve to recognize this deeper level of Awareness, as this very Awareness is never absent, being the constant conscious presence in which all thoughts and sensations appear. For without this presence we would not be aware of any thought or sensation.[29] Also, as this is the only constant factor that has been present throughout (and witnessed) our entire lives, whereas our thoughts/sensations (mind/bodies) are always changing, then this Awareness is what we truly are at the most fundamental level.

So now, there being nothing to achieve, find or acquire, one can totally 'let go' and relax deeply into this Awareness …

Now notice the sensations (and feelings) in, and on the surface of, the body. Sink into these sensations, really luxuriate in them as much as possible. Ignore all other sense impressions and thoughts except these sensations. Realize that these occur, are detected by the

---

[29] From *Beyond The Separate Self* p.85

nervous system, processed by the brain and are then 'seen' by Awareness – i.e. you become 'aware' of them.

So the body/mind (itself a manifestation of cosmic energy – the beloved) is an instrument through which Awareness- Consciousness at rest, the lover – can feel the external world – Consciousness in motion, the beloved.

If this is continued with for some time one starts to feel the bliss of embodiment – the rhythmic beating of the heart, the blood pumping through the veins, the air on one's face, the warmth in one's feet, sensations of the touching points where the body is in contact with the ground (cushion, pillow, mattress etc.) and so on. The more one can sink into, and luxuriate in, these sensations the stronger the practice becomes.

Just continue with this luxuriating, aware of the fact that this is Awareness itself (Consciousness at rest – the lover), which is what in essence you are, using the body/mind as a medium to feel Its manifestation the physical world – cosmic energy – Consciousness in motion – the beloved. Thus the lover is able to sense its own manifestation – the beloved.

The bliss can be quite subtle at first, so if you are not aware of this then start with the feeling of ease and comfort as the body sinks more deeply into its support. Notice the absolute freedom of nothing to achieve, seek for or desire, as That which you could want is always already here – Pure Awareness itself! First focus on the touching points where the body comes into contact with its supporting surface. Deeply feel the sensation of letting go into this and the relaxation and comfort associated with this. Then come to the effortless rising and falling of the chest and abdomen as your body gently calmly breathes itself … feel the ease of this for some time. Next notice the soft caress of your shirt, or blouse, as your chest and abdomen move up into and then down away from this. Feel the gentle joy of all this for a period before becoming aware of the slightly cooling air on the face and hands and then of the subtle throbbing of the circulation as the blood flows around the body.

If thoughts arise just let them come and go whilst simply returning to this balmy bliss of being in the body. As the practice continues these thoughts will lessen, especially if you remain identified with this Awareness which is witnessing all of the bodily sensations as they ebb and they flow. Also, the mind will find it easy to return to the bliss, as this will be 'tastier' than any thoughts which arise and the mind is programmed to seek for pleasure. This will lead to the bliss slowly magnifying as the distractions lessen and the sensations will seem to intensify as you become more deeply aware of them.

Continue this for as long as you are comfortable and you can mentally repeat 'feeling you my love' with each 'wave' of sensation, or with the breath, if this appeals to you. For you are indeed the 'lover' (Pure Awareness – Consciousness at rest) feeling the 'beloved' - Its manifestation, the universe, cosmic energy, Consciousness in motion. Also this the body/mind is a wonderful instrument with its extensive nervous system (system of nerves which pervade the whole body) and other senses.

Alternatively, you can mentally repeat 'the bliss of the beloved' as you feel the ease and comfort of these sensations, which I find slowly increases the bliss as it is repeated. I suspect that there is an increase of endorphin release during this whole process which is also stimulated by the continual mental repetition of the words 'love' or 'bliss'. It is well known that mind states affect the bodily functions (and feelings) and I posit that this is a classic example of this occurring. At all events the bliss increases as the mind stills and the utter relaxation deepens…

As you arise, from this practice of deeply blissful relaxation, take your time slowly 'coming to' and try to maintain this 'loving feeling' towards your surroundings for as long as possible.

Then:

Nurturing The Bliss of Awakening

> When awake we can feel the bliss,
>
> Of living, which we generally miss.
>
> Resulting in loving one and all,
>
> On whomsoe'er one's eye may fall[30].

This is a classic win-win situation where the mind is engaged doing something it finds to be easy and really enjoys, whilst revealing that the mind/body is indeed a conduit through which Awareness can enjoy Its own manifestation. There is also no referencing to an illusory 'individual self' as identifying with, and as, Pure Awareness is the prerequisite to commencing (and staying engaged in) the whole practice.

The results of this will eventually permeate your entire day so this bliss may be readily re-accessed at any time by sitting, or lying, quietly and bringing your attention to it. It also makes seemingly stressful situations less so, as the underlying bliss (or peace) negates the negative emotions as they attempt to arise; or even prevents them arising at all!

To give a personal example of this:

---

[30] From *Poetry From Beyond The Separate Self, The Best of All Worlds* p.69

Nurturing The Bliss of Awakening

I am an Englishman who has now been living in Australia for over forty years ... what luck! However, as I was from a cool to cold climate I am not keen on very hot weather and tended to overheat (physically and then mentally) quite easily when the mercury rises above 30C (86F) and I am working outside. Luckily (my life is full of this) I am self-employed in an indoor occupation and the pottery is shady and cool even on the hottest days. So, when I have outdoor work to do, we have an old macadamia plantation over 10 acres, I normally choose cool days for this. Yesterday, however, our old campervan chose not to start so I called the local roadside assistance for help. By the time he arrived at midday it was 35C (95F) in the shade and over 40C (104F) in the sun. We spent over an hour and a half outside (with no shade) attempting to start and then towing the van out. It was parked under the kiln-shelter, down an exposed narrow drive with steep sides, which contains a 150 degree bend, and was thus very tricky to extricate. I noticed that, although I did get very hot physically, I stayed calm and cheerful throughout the whole process ... which would have been impossible before my Awakening and the subsequent cultivation of this.

I also accepted the fact that our seven day trip, to various 'highland' national parks, would have to be abandoned, without any resistance ... actually I went home, cooled down, and then did a yoga-nidra. This is a very powerful relaxation technique which my wife and I have been doing, on a daily basis, for over 30 years and which can change (in fact is guaranteed to after enough practice) one's head space from agitated to serene in less than half an hour. In fact, this has many similarities with the practice I have outlined above, although it has other components and does not focus on the bliss.

Twelve – Awakening and Suffering

A general discussion considering how Awakening relieves the suffering of the one who 'awakens' and can be used to alleviate the suffering of 'others' and the world.

Here is a post I found on an internet group devoted to nonduality:

> It's one of those spiralling questions, all the way in and out of form in the short time we have here in physical bodies. "How the hell is Pure Awareness and this nonduality Shite in anyway helping the suffering on the planet? Isn't it absenteeism? Isn't it neglect of sheer human responsibility? Isn't this perceptive elation actually escapism - falling into a space of collective denial of the horror which is here - that space where great men do "nothing"?

This is a serious question which has many facets and is not illuminated by the use of such emotive language. There are many things to consider:

a. How does Awakening alleviate the suffering of the 'awakener'?

b. What kind of suffering does this alleviate?

c. How can one help 'others' to go beyond this type of suffering?

d. What are the motives of those who inflict suffering on others?

e. How can one influence these to desist?

f. What is the best way to help reduce the environmental degradation of the planet ... which leads to much suffering for those affected by rising sea levels etc.?

g. What can one do to help those whose suffering is caused by the actions of others?

I will consider with each of these in turn, mostly using segments from previous essays as I have written on them all at various times, but have not put them together in this way before.

a. How does Awakening alleviate the suffering of the 'awakener'?

> Once Awakening has taken place then anxiety and unnecessary mental suffering disappear, for these are caused by misidentifying oneself as a separate object in a world of separate objects. This causes us to see each other, and the world, through a murky filter of self-interest, self-concern, self-promotion, self-aggrandizement, self-loathing, the list is almost endless. It is this world-view that causes the anxiety and mental suffering based on concern for the future and feeling we are bound by the past. On Awakening one discovers that there truly is no separate self and so this filter is removed allowing us to see the world 'as it is' with no self-concern for the future or past.[31]

The fact that the small self is just an illusion can be seen by investigating the nature of our moment to moment existence, see appendix 1. When this is carried out we become 'aware of Awareness' which the Buddha regarded as the 'first factor of enlightenment'. The second factor he gives is 'investigation of the way' which is exactly what this appendix does, resulting in discovering that, at the deepest level, **we are Awareness itself**! The outcome of this is, at this deeper level, we relate to others in a much more loving, wholesome way, for it becomes clear that there is in fact no separation between ourselves and others, as we share the same constant conscious subjective presence.[32]

b. What kind of suffering does this alleviate?

I distinguish between pain, mental and physical, which is endemic to life in the body/mind and mental suffering which is caused by identifying oneself as a separate object in a world of such. So, some pain is unavoidable but all mental suffering is avoidable by correct identification. To give a rather radical example of this:

Sri Ramakrishna, Sri Ramana Maharshi and Nisargadatta Maharaj are three of the most famous self-realized masters of

---

[31] *Freedom From Anxiety and Needless Suffering*, p.5
[32] *Beyond The Separate Self*, p.13.

Awakening and Suffering

the last two hundred years. They all died of cancer but did not mentally suffer although the body was in great pain, as they were not identified with it ... just regarding it like a damaged suit of clothes that they were about to discard. Here is an excerpt from The Gospel of Ramakrishna:

> The Master's body was being racked with indescribable pain. The devotees could not bear the sight of this illness; but somehow the Master made them forget his suffering. He sat there, his face beaming as if there were no trace of illness in his throat.[33]

When asked why a devotee of God should suffer so he replied 'it is the body that suffers'.

This does not mean that we should not look after the body for it is our temporary dwelling and the instrument through which we, as Pure Awareness, act in, engage with, and enjoy, the world. That is it is the conduit through which Consciousness can 'know Itself' when in manifestation as the material world (Cosmic Energy ... Consciousness in motion). Thus we need to keep it in the best possible condition to maximize its potential, whilst being in pain reduces our ability to enjoy life ... thus lessening its usefulness. Also, at the surface level, we all like to be pain free with a healthy functional body.

---

[33] The Gospel of Ramakrishna, tr by Sw. Nikhilananda, 1942, Ramakrishna-Vivekananda Centre, New York, p.969

A good example of unavoidable mental pain is that caused by the loss of a loved one which is natural, but leads to unnecessary mental suffering when one 'stews' on this and it becomes self-pity. This can only occur when one is identified with the 'small self', that is as a separate object, rather than the Pure Awareness (Consciousness) that underlies everything.

Whereas, an example of unnecessary suffering caused by misidentification is 'the mental pain of not achieving enough in the world and leaving your mark (or at least blaming yourself for not)', for in Reality there is no separate self who is the doer …[34]

c. How can one help 'others' to go beyond this type of suffering?

By helping them to go *Beyond the Separate Self* (see book of same name) providing pointers to Awakening, encouraging others to 'awaken' in every way possible. Another way to reduce suffering is to create as much joy, for oneself and 'others' as one can, for more on this see the earlier chapter 'Compassion and Spirituality'.

d. What are the motives of those who inflict suffering on others?

---

[34] *The Happiness That Needs Nothing*, p.99-102

Awakening and Suffering

It says in the Upanishads that all acts are performed by The Self (Awareness, Brahman) for the sake of The Self and love of The Self.[35] Their 'flavour' is caused by the relative wisdom or ignorance of the 'actor', the instrument, committing them. So it seems to me that 'good' and 'evil' acts stem from the same motivation and their outward expression is dependent on the degree of Awareness that the perpetrator exhibits. The former by those who exhibit some degree of Awakening, wisdom, and identification with the Totality (Consciousness, Brahman); whereas, the latter are more likely to be committed by those who are relatively 'asleep', ignorant, or identified as a separate object in a universe of such. For then they are liable to treat others as 'objects' for this is what they think they are!

The natural corollary to this is that if we awaken, by realizing that we are Pure Awareness (the constant conscious subjective presence), and cultivate this Awakening by remaining identified as (and with) This, then we tend to become a force for 'good', peace, harmony, positivity and creativity. Whereas, if we remain asleep, identified as an object in a universe of objects, we could become a force for 'evil', violence, discord, negativity and destructivity.[36]

---

[35] This is self-evident as we are all manifestations of Consciousness, Brahman, whether we know it or not.
[36] *Awakening and Beyond*, p.152

e. How can one influence these to desist?

> By pointing out the causes of their own suffering and helping them to go *Beyond the Separate Self* (see book of same name) providing pointers to Awakening, encouraging them to 'awaken' in every way possible. Without a change of identification there will be no motive to change one's behaviour, but when one awakens to the fact that one is Pure Awareness then, it follows that this is known to be the case for all sentient beings. At this level there is truly no separation between oneself and any other being, and this naturally leads to compassion.[37] Which entails treating others in the same way that one would wish to be treated by others.

f. What is the best way to help reduce the environmental degradation of the planet ... which leads to much suffering for those affected by rising sea levels etc.?

> The major cause of this problem is greed and the expectation that there will always be more and more. What is needed is a paradigm shift away from personal interest and towards acting for the common good, which will not occur as long as we identify ourselves as separate individual beings living in a hostile universe.

---

[37] *Beyond The Separate Self*, p.94

Awakening and Suffering

In fact identifying with the deeper level of our being, Pure Awareness, enhances our humanity immeasurably and if this were the common condition then all instances of man's inhumanity to his (or her) fellow man would be consigned to history. For, this deeper identification leads to joy, peace, love of all beings (in fact of the whole of existence) and true selfless compassion. This is because at this level there is no separation as all of manifestation is seen to be just the play of consciousness, cosmic energy, movements in consciousness itself.[38] When this realization occurs then the lust for power naturally diminishes and greed is a thing of the past.

This would truly be the best of all worlds for humanity, as we all seek joy and peace; the problem is in general that we look in the wrong place, the external world, rather than the centre of our own being. So to create this Utopia we need to commit to identifying with the deeper level of Pure Awareness, and to encourage those around us to do the same. The more we become established in this level of identification the closer we come to the peak of human existence and thus the more we enhance our true humanity.[39]

So, in conclusion, I maintain that the solution to the environmental crisis is for humanity to 'awaken' by becoming

---
[38] *Ibid* p.113
[39] *Ibid* p 115

Awakening and Suffering

aware of, and identifying with, Awareness itself. After which we live more simply, as we are not seeking for happiness in material possessions, for we discover that happiness is truly (and always) within. In this way our carbon footprint will be naturally lowered and we will be more inclined to eschew self-interest and act for the common good.[40]

g. What can one do to help those whose suffering is caused by the actions of others?

With regard to suffering that is caused by external circumstances that are beyond one's control, we can at least empathize with those affected; join, assist and donate to groups that help these if we are able, and aid anyone that we meet that is in this category.

---

[40] *Awakening and Beyond*, p. 21-24

Thirteen – The Myth of The Awakened State

Debunks the myth that when one is 'awake' then one becomes a 'stone buddha' showing no seemingly negative emotions.

The Myth of The Awakened State

There seems to be a myth that an awakened being should be always in a state of complete equanimity, rather like a 'stone buddha'. This was reinforced, for me, by my family members in the following circumstances. Firstly, by my sister who had not seen me for years but had been receiving my emails, so that when we met she judged my behaviour by her conception of a 'perfect being'. This caused her to continually criticize my behaviour when I exhibited natural human states such as irritation or exasperation. Secondly, by my son when we were playing golf and I expressed my frustration at the state of the greens, which had been heavily sanded and made putting well nigh impossible. I expressed my dissatisfaction and commented that it was 'hardly worth even lining the puts up' whereupon he countered with 'you spend so much time meditating and yet you still get upset …' Finally, yesterday, my wife and a friend were in the campervan and she was inexpertly attempting to help me reverse out of a tight situation. When I expressed my disapproval the friend commented that this was hardly the action of a buddha which my wife reinforced by saying 'yes it's all bullshit!' Now, if by this she had meant that the idea that an awakened being wouldn't criticize another is bullshit, I would agree with her. However, she seemed to be indicating the reverse, that if you criticize another this indicates that you aren't 'awake', which may actually well have been the case in this incident … see last paragraph.

Other instances spring to mind, such as a friend criticizing me for walking out of a very violent movie, rather than accepting it with equanimity. For more on this see 'Detachment or Engagement?' in *The Happiness That Needs Nothing.* So a word of warning, to all of you who have 'awakened' and are thinking of 'coming out' so as to help others by providing your unique set of pointers (to Awakening), you must be prepared for the brickbats that will be hurled at you. Luckily they will be of virtually no 'weight' as you won't take them personally (for you will have discovered that there is, in truth, no 'separate person') but it's still not pleasant. Actually they provide an ideal opportunity to test whether you are still 'awake', for if you find them painful then you have probably nodded off and need to reawaken, which can be easily done by noticing that they are just ephemeral objects appearing in the Pure Awareness that you 'are'.

Actually if you look at accounts of historical 'awakened beings' you will find many accounts of them being angry, upset, critical etc. Ramakrishna springs to mind as a wonderfully liberated being who vividly expressed all emotions - joy, delight, anger, grief etc. So Awakening does not make one immune to the seemingly 'negative' emotions, but it does mean that they arise and subside quite spontaneously without any clinging to them. Awakening can have other wonderful outcomes such as:

Transcending all existential angst about the future and fate of the body/mind.

The end of all needless suffering caused by identifying oneself as an object.

No longer regarding 'others' as objects and thus not labelling them.

Not taking criticism personally as there is no 'person'.

No longer seeing the world through the murky filter of the small self.

Fearlessness – living spontaneously without fear running in the mind as a background program.

As well as these, there are those already given in *Beyond The Separate Self*:

> Compassion. Once one sees that, at the deepest level, one is Pure Awareness it follows that this is the case for all sentient beings. At this level there is truly no separation between oneself and any other being, and this naturally leads to compassion.

Discrimination between the 'real' and the 'unreal'. This level of Pure Awareness is classified as the 'real' in that it is constant, unchanging and unaffected by any 'thing', Whereas the level of manifestation, of things, is classified as 'unreal' in that it is always changing and is governed by the laws of cause and effect. Once one becomes completely identified with Pure Awareness then this becomes obvious and no discrimination is needed.

Love of God and one's fellow man. The word God means consciousness which has two states, at rest (Pure Awareness), and in motion (manifestation). In this there is truly no separation as the essence (and the ground of) of all that exists, is consciousness, and true love is only present where there is no separation; in fact true love is 'no separation'… The Christian idea that 'god is Love' points to this, and love of one's fellow man naturally follows on from the realization of no separation.

Contentment, and remaining fundamentally unaffected by external circumstances. Pure Awareness is always in this condition, and thus complete identification with Awareness naturally leads to this… So irritations, upsets, anger etc., arise in this and subside back into this leaving it unaffected.

The degree to which these manifest depends on how established one is in 'Awakening' – that is how much one flip/flops between the 'awakened' and 'asleep' states. Their expression will vary depending on character and personality which are unique for each of us. The point is that there is no fixed model for the behaviour of an 'awakened' being and thus, up to a point, one cannot use this to judge their degree of 'Awakening'. Also this means that any attempt to mimic the behaviour of any such being, in the hope that this will induce some degree (or appearance) of 'Awakening' is futile.

One final point is that I have never claimed to be totally 'awakened' as I am still subject to the occasional flip/flop. Luckily this always produces unnecessary mental suffering which is used as a trigger to reawaken, a strategy I encourage all of my readers to employ. Either by immediately seeing that one is aware of this suffering which is just an object that has appeared in this Awareness, and that at the essential level one is this Awareness; or by reinvestigating this momentary experience, as given in the appendix, which again reveals that one is Awareness itself.

Fourteen – Reason - Its Uses Before and After Awakening

Discusses whether after Awakening one loses the use of reason and whether this is useful in the Awakening process.

Reason – Its Uses Before and After Awakening

The original discussion post by PS.

The main danger of realizing unity, is to abandon reason and just pedal along with hands off the steering handle bars. Look, mom, no hands! Reason is the leash that keep words and actions in check. Steer your words, least you become an enlightened fool.

• DL: Is not reason, essentially, a survival mechanism for the separate self? And is not reason unable to comprehend paradox and contradiction? These would seem to be two 'reasons' why reason needs to be left behind at some point. Not that it doesn't still remain to serve-- but it would seem that it does need to be let go of, let loose.

• DS: PS, a melting is a changeful occurrence within that which does not change.

I have had such experience, where the veil dissolved and the whole of creation folded into me.

• DC: Any description of Awareness is not Awareness.

• DS: Any description, being knowable, is known.

Reason – Its Uses Before and After Awakening

- NJ: Daniel I agree that reason shouldn't be left out of inquiry / scrutiny. Not so much about your definition of reason

- DC: Ok so is Awareness knowable or are you aware of knowing?

- DS: I am aware that I am aware. Awareness is not an object.

- Me: Spot on! The mind is much more efficient when uncluttered by the illusory 'small self' and its opinions, self-concern, self-promotion, self-aggrandizement, self-hate, self-interest etc.... the list is endless. It is a wonderful problem-solving device which is hampered by the constantly running background program of 'me,me,me'. When this disappears due to the established realization of 'no self' it reveals its full potential.

- DC: Oh Ya...

- DS: Yes. The mind / intellect is an amazing instrument, capable of the greatest realizations and reason.

If you doubt its power, just look at how efficiently it keeps people in ignorance.

- Me: BTW PS is not enamoured by discussions on Awareness, as is shown by his recent comment on my latest post : 'Colin, you are hopelessly attached to Awareness. Give up that ghost!'

- DC: Hmm...How might one let go Awareness...would one know they has succeeded?

- DS: Yes, it seems PS is trapped on board the dualistic 'experiential' path.

- Me: And what a wonderful tool it (the mind) can be in the search for Awakening, when one does not identify with it as who one 'is'.

- DS: The instrument of God's intelligence.

- Me: Yes indeed!!

My reply to PS was: 'I am Awareness ... every time I look there It is, the only constant in the ever-flowing sea of experience... Although you could argue that It's a ghost in that you can't see it with your eyes! More like the ghostly Presence that's all pervading ...
No attachment necessary ... and impossible to detach from the essence of all!!'

Reason – Its Uses Before and After Awakening

- DC: If it is the instrument and the instrument is not separate from God...

- Me: Nothing is, or can be!!

Nonduality ... Only God, The Tao, Allah, Jehovah, The Void, Awareness, Brahman, Rigpa, Consciousness ... call it what you will.

- DS: I would strike the void from your list, because it is known.

- Me: Aware Nothingness is limitless, and can never be fully 'known' ...
Although we can 'know' that it is the Source, Ground and Dissolution of all that is ...

- DL: Reason is a sense gate, like the eyes and ears. It gives a picture of reality, never the thing itself. No reason to abandon the eyes, or the reasoning mind. But attachment to the picture is the problem. Similar with beliefs. Beliefs are no problem, attachment to beliefs obscures reality. The issue is always attachment, never the vehicle itself.

- DS: Our problem is not that we aren't already the eternal and limitless aware self, but that we fail to see or doubt the truth of this.

Reason – Its Uses Before and After Awakening

- Me: To address PS's original comment, see my latest post (Oneness) which relies on reason and rationality ... and is about unity itself. It also posits that Awareness, Consciousness at Rest, is the 'ground' of all, so I'm not expecting a 'like' from PS!

- DS: Maybe after PS melts, we can cool him off into a more agreeable form.

- Me: No he'll just merge into the ocean and we won't be able to find him ...

- DL: Actually, reason is irrelevant to unity, or realization. It's neither good nor bad--it just doesn't apply. Reason only supplies answers, and solutions to problems. But realization is not the answer to any question, or the solution to a problem. It's simply the seeing of present reality, which is eternally without question or problem.

- NJ: Daniel I wouldn't say reason is irrelevant with respect to inquiry and realization because if you're using inquiry you almost inevitably use reason. It helps to clear wrong views…

- Me: Fully agree Neil

- NJ: Any reason why?

Reason – Its Uses Before and After Awakening

- Me: If you read any of my books or articles you will see that I recommend directly investigating ones moment to moment experience which reveals that one is Awareness . I have developed a framework for this that uses reason alongside insight.

After much more discussion to which I was not party ...

- Me: So many different 'takes' on unity ... the 'Truth' is ineffable indeed! But thanks to Jerry Katz for creating this group and providing the platform where we can all try to 'eff the ineffable'.
For within the attempted 'effing' more is revealed of the limitless ... and the discussion can go on forever without 'getting to the bottom (or top) of It! But it sure is fun trying ...

As Gangaji says 'one day I'll manage to say it ...' Actually I've got her to thank for she gave us (participants in a seven day retreat with her in 1996) the task of 'saying it' and told us never to give up until we had managed it! What a boon for I shall be trying until 'I' (this body/mind) shuffle off this mortal coil ...

- GJ: Until it's not

- Me: Or is ...

Reason – Its Uses Before and After Awakening

- Me: It's all the same ...

- CL: *♫•♪*♫ From "Rhiannon" Fleetwood Mac, Stevie Nicks, "

...All the same

All the same

All the same, Rhiannon

All the same (x3)

Take me with you to the sky

All the same

All the same, Rhiannon

All the same (x3)

Take me with you to the sky

Dreams unwind

Love's a state of mind"

- Me: A state of mind and much more ...

- DL: this task of "saying it" is a curious thing. I feel that's what everyone is always doing--trying to "say it." But most won't acknowledge this, and instead pretend they're doing something else. Like when Colin takes a photo, or makes a pot. He's trying to say this thing that can't be said--in the most perfect and eloquent way he can. I make drawings, music, internet comments, and brush my teeth, etc. But it's all just this perpetual attempt to formulate this unformable, unsayable thing. Nothing else to do here, that I can find.

- DC: In the end a poet and musician feel there is something more they could have said.

- Me: There's always more ... or less!

- GJ: Birds sing together at dawn and sunset. On the other side of the universe, their music could be creating whole new planets. With so much speaking, we - who are so close to the source - are hardly able to hear even our own articulation.

Me: And yet, and yet ...

As we are, in essence Awareness Itself it is theoretically possible that one could access everything that appears in Consciousness ... Consider 'Morphic Resonance' the theory that Rupert Sheldrake developed to explain almost simultaneous major discoveries. In 1922, William Ogburn and Dorothy Thomas discovered 148 scientific discoveries that fit a pattern referred to by science historians as multiples. A multiple is said to occur when a particular scientific discovery is found to have emerged in multiple geographic locations either simultaneously or within the same time period, but independently of each other. The following are just a few examples of such "multiples":

Joule, Colding, Thomson and Helmholz each articulated the law of the conservation of energy independently of one another in 1847.
There appear to have been at least six different individuals who invented the thermometer.
Nine individuals each claimed to have invented the telescope.
Multiple inventors in the U.S. and England developed the typewriter, each unaided by the others.
Fulton, Jouffroy, Rumsey, Stevens and Symington each claimed exclusive invention of the steamboat.
Calculus was discovered not only by Leibniz, but by Newton as well.
Decimal fractions were developed independently by three different mathematicians.
Carl Wilhelm Scheele discovered oxygen in Sweden 1773, and Joseph Priestly discovered it independently in England a year later.
Two researchers in France, Charles Cros and Louis Ducos du Hauron, invented color photography independently of one another.
Galileo in Italy, Fabricius in Holland, Harriott in England, and Scheiner in Germany all independently discovered sunspots in 1611.
These observations, along with many other studies, discoveries and even spiritual texts not mentioned here, paint the picture of a shared

informational field to which we all subtly entrain. This refined and often unconscious or intuitive mutual resonance—between field and organism—appears to help us cognize the world in which we live.

Fifteen – Internet Discussion About The Absolute

Considers the question of writing about The Absolute and also Its essential nature.

Internet Discussion About The Absolute

In reply to an article I posted on an internet group, devoted to nonduality, entitled 'Why Write About the Ineffable' (from *Awareness of Awareness – The Open Way*) here is the discussion that followed:

- RM: I saw myself as golden luminous light flowing out from my third eye in meditation; had noticed this light before but it was a white light in the beginning which I thought was ectoplasm.

- Me: Radiant Pure Awareness ... The source, 'ground' and dissolution of all being.

- GJ: The problem about writing about the Effable is that it becomes ineffable the moment you try and define it.

- XA : I go for the "pointing toward" reason... that others may also discover the truth of being. (As the reason for writing about the ineffable.)

- RM: Ineffable (in effable); it is both together as one.

- Me: As the Bee Gees put it 'It's only words and words are all I have....'

- Me: Apart from my 'being ' that is ... which is ineffable...

• DR : Everything is unworded, nothing is the word.... Language guides everything from the void of nothing. .... Man is the existence of everything and is nothing in all that we are. ... To name nothing is the state everything.(thus unworded)... What is empty must be filled. Nothing in Everything.... A state of nothing never lacks order. ... A state of nothing is a state of single-mindedness were the unconscious is unaware of the bug on his skin. ...

Tao WoW

• Me: All is the Tao

• DR : Exactly, the void gives form to all, yet is formlessness within itself

• DR : The Void within the Tao and Dao(Dharma)

• Me: Pure Aware Nothingness, Consciousness at rest, in which all 'things' are cosmic energy and thus ephemeral movements in That.

• DR : Sahaj Samadhi one is Total (Order/Nothingness) while Awareness is living operator of what is. Beyond what is, is yonder be all no-things becoming into things. Thus the appearance of Reality, comes to us as Awareness before Projection;; thus all rises from the Tao.

remember, if Awareness has confusion...why is that?? This remains a mystery...

- Me: Arising in That, abiding in That and subsiding back into That.

- DR : that is opposed by this

- Me: No confusion in Awareness!!!

- Me: That is This and This is That!

- DR: If there is a foreign Awareness from the mind being altered, then which is the Pure Awareness? Is it still Awareness of Self or is the state altered to Pure Self? With Self as the root of the Awareness

- Me: Awareness is always pure for no thing (ephemeral movement) can taint it, as they all arise in and subside back into That ... leaving It unchanged.

- CL: Didn't read but the first paragraph - but what came to mind is needing a thorn to remove a thorn.

- DR: If my Awareness is Awake, and yours is Asleep, then who is the one Wrong in the dream? For if I dream my Awareness, then how does the come to an Awareness that is awake? Does a single seed contain the Awareness of all? I think to be awake, is to see aidya in self and others

All in all, Awareness must "BE" to be that.

- Me: The Constant Conscious Subjective Presence ... not personal but animating all.

The seeming 'personal' Awareness is just a limited (by the mind) incidence of Pure Awareness , where the mind focuses on something appearing in Awareness.

Just another ephemeral movement in That. ...

- DR: This moved that, so that moved this

- DR: If there is Pure Awareness and Awareness, that is a dichotomy already and split from what you said as Awareness always is whole. Imagine two bubbles, each its own Awareness coming together to merge into one new bubble, so twice the double condition of one

- Me: They are always One ... for Pure Awareness contains (and Is) all...

There is never any separation ... just the appearance of separation! Not two (bubbles or anything else) ... nonduality

- RM: Colin, I believe your motives are pure! So why not create some kind of Teleclass and offer it to your subscribers? Charge a fee you think is fair and see who signs up. Many years ago I wrote an online best seller on marketing. And then I offered 3 and 6 month and then ultimately 1-year programs all via teleconference to those buyers. When I wrote my book, The Unstuck Process, I gave away 3,000 ebooks in exchange for a name and email. Then I promoted a 6-session course about this process to my list and 21 people signed up. Why not you? I'm willing to bet that many on your list would appreciate a course and the chance for direct contact. That is service, not selling.

- Me: There are a few reasons:

Firstly I live in the 'bush' as they call it in these parts and have very bad internet connection so no teleconferencing ... Secondly what I write about is so simple that it should not require a 'course' but just some pointing and one's own direct 'seeing' based on one's own investigations. I have had many e-mails from readers who have managed this as a result of reading (any of) my books. Thirdly anyone is welcome to contact me by e-mail (colin108@dodo.com.au) and I will help them through any difficulties they are having for as long as it takes ... Once again I have had successful communications with many of my readers resulting in them identifying with, and as, Pure Awareness. Fourthly I have no need to generate any income, for the Australian Old Age Pension is quite adequate. Fifthly I am a lazy bugger who lives in a wonderful environment and am loath to leave it for any length of time ... to do a lecture tour for example. Sixthly, once again what I am pointing to is so incredibly simple that I do not believe this to be necessary.

- Me: In reply to DR: you are making it all much too complicated, but I earnestly believe that we are not at odds, just 'saying it' it differently...

In the end It is ineffable but It so fills (is) my whole being that it oozes out in words, poems, song, joy, love etc ...

None of which ever do it justice!!

- RM: Great answer, Colin. You are a treasure. Y'know it might be simple, but took me about 50 years to find it! So simple is a relative term. And if it was as simple as tying your shoes, the whole world would be awake! Cheers, RM

Me: Yes I know, it took me 30 years, but only because I had never been pointed in the right direction! It is as simple as tying your shoes ... but most people are not interested in anything as complicated as tying laces! They'd rather have a 'slip on' (mis)identity which they can slip into when they need one ...

- RM: Colin, I'll take you up on emailing, but not now as I'm off to bed as it's midnight here!

- Me: Sweet Dreams...

- GM: Effable way of describing the Ineffable, Beautiful

- Me: Thank you, but as Gangaji says 'one day I'll manage to say it ...' Actually I've got her to thank for she gave us (participants in a seven day retreat with her in 1996) the task of 'saying it' and told us never to give up until we had managed it! What a boon for I shall be trying until 'I' (this body/mind) shuffle off this mortal coil ... and as I said in the original post this should keep me awake for when one is contemplating and writing about Awareness this keeps one 'aware of Awareness' and thus awake.

Also the more one contemplates and investigates This the more is found, for This is infinite and the recognition of oneself as This has untold ramifications ... So never any end to this wonderful inquiry!

Internet Discussion About The Absolute

- JK: the original question isn't separate from the answer. the answer is Awareness. often people go to a teacher or a satsang with questions and they watch them dissolve and aren't sure why. it's because something about the presence is the answer.

- Me: As one becomes aware of the presence (Awareness), and realises the significance of This, all questions dissolve ... leaving only further discoveries to occur as inquiry deepens.

Awareness of Awareness - The Open Way! Open to all, requiring no guru, auspicious birth, special knowledge or abilities ...

Just requiring a few friendly pointers in the right direction and total commitment to what is revealed ...

- DR: "right direction" under whose imposition? and directions are relative to initial self realization

- Me: There are many avenues for enquiry it's just a matter of finding the one that one resonates with. Different strokes for different folks as they say....

- PS: Colin, you are hopelessly attached to Awareness. Give up that ghost!

Internet Discussion About The Absolute

- Me: I am Awareness ... every time I look there It is, the only constant in the ever-flowing sea of experience... Although you could argue that It's a ghost in that you can't see it with your eyes! More like the ghostly Presence that's all pervading ...

No attachment necessary ... and impossible to detach from the essence of all!!

- DR: How was your Awareness before you recognized your Self?

- Me: Do you mean how has self-recognition changed my life? Awareness doesn't change ... 'my Awareness' is just my mind noticing the thoughts and sensations that are occurring.

DR: Thank you for showing Awareness is always, seems like it is always in every moment, so hence there is always only Awareness, even regardless of formlessness or form. My apology, apart of me in esprit.

Sixteen – Awareness - The Myth

Discusses the Myth that Awareness is only concerned with one 'thing' noticing, or becoming aware, of another. Whereas, this is only a very limited form of the Awareness that underlies the whole of Reality.

Awareness - The Myth

Most people seem not to understand the term 'Awareness' and subscribe to the myth that this is confined to an object and is manifest when this object notices another one. E.g. 'The cat became aware of the mouse' or 'I was awoken by the sound of a plane entering my field of Awareness'. This is the reason why materialists regard Awareness as a property of the brain and that this is necessary for its existence, or that Awareness only exists when an experience takes place i.e. one becomes 'aware' of something. For example:

> 'There cannot be any Awareness unless there is one who is aware and, what/who is it that is aware? The brain of course! Before the brain existed & upon its death there was no & will be no Awareness.'

In reply to this misconceptions I wrote the following in the introduction of my book 'Awareness of Awareness – The Open Way':

> The phrase 'awareness of Awareness' utilises two, related but different, meanings and for this reason I have used a capital letter (when using this expression) for the second one so that they may be easily distinguished in what follows[41].

---

[41] In general, throughout all of my books, whenever I use the word 'awareness' I am using this as Awareness (The Totality which is 'aware' of all) unless it is in the phrase 'awareness of Awareness' which the following discussion addresses.

The first occurrence (awareness) is synonymous with mindfulness, that is 'seeing' with the mind, or keeping (something) in the mind. It also means 'becoming conscious of', noticing, or perceiving, as in 'I became aware of ...' This is the normal everyday usage as in the OED definition of 'aware' – *having knowledge or perception of ...*

So the term 'awareness of Awareness' means becoming conscious, or having knowledge or perception, of Awareness. We now need to define this Awareness which is simply the total 'seeing' and perceiving (or seer and perceiver) of everything detected by the mind and senses, whereas Awareness (becoming aware of) is the partial 'seeing' of those thoughts/sensations on which the mind is focussed, or which are noticed. So these are not different, awareness just being a limited version (or incidence) of Awareness.

This is easy to directly experience by closing one's eyes and seeing whether you can simultaneously be 'aware of' (notice) all of the thoughts/mental images and sensations that are occurring. This is found to be impossible and yet these are all there in Awareness, which becomes apparent when one focuses one's mind on , or turns one's mind to, any of them…. and there they are!

In fact Awareness saturates the whole of manifestation, from electrons changing their behaviour when (aware of) being observed[42], cells responding to (aware of) changing environments, white corpuscles attacking viruses they detect (are aware of) in the blood, moulds moving towards (when aware of) foods placed near them and so on...

It has actually been shown that the only time that electrons ever manifest as particles is when we are looking at them, otherwise they manifests as waves[43]. It has also been shown that this coalescence into particles occurs before it is theoretically possible for any information to have passed between the observer and the observed! Thus this Awareness, by the electron of being observed, is not a case of it 'seeing' that an observer was present ... that is to say that it is not an example of the first definition of Awareness, given above. It is actually a case of the electron 'knowing' that the observer was present because they are part of one continuum, as is everything[44], and thus no information needed to be traded!

Neils Bohr showed that subatomic particles are not independent 'things' but were part of an indivisible system and to think of them as otherwise was meaningless[45]. David Bohm through his experiments on plasma

---

[42] See the 'double-slit' experiment.
[43] M. Talbot, *The Holographic Universe*', 1996, London, p.34
[44] Ibid, p.48
[45] Ibid, p.37

discovered that 'electrons stopped behaving like individuals and started behaving as if they were part of a larger interconnected whole ... resulting in entire oceans of particles each behaving as if it knew what untold trillions of others were doing.'[46]

This is a case of the second definition of Awareness where so-called 'things' exist in a 'field of Awareness' and are 'aware' of the behaviour of other 'things' in this 'field'; not by faculties which 'see' these other things (the first definition) but by the fact of no separation in which all are the same 'thing' (or system)! In the same way that if you shine a laser on any part of a photographic plate, on which a holographic image has been stored, it will produce the whole holograph ... even if the plate has been cut into many pieces. In this case this information (needed to produce the image) is contained at every point on the plate and, in the same way, all information is accessible at every point in the 'system' given above. In fact Bohm went even further and indicated that, 'at the subquantum level, location ceased to exist! All points in space became equal to all other points in space, and it was meaningless to speak of anything as being separate from anything else. Physicists call this property 'nonlocality'.[47]

He also posits that:
> Consciousness is present in ... all matter which is perhaps why plasmas posses some of the traits of living things. Life and

---
[46] Ibid, p.38
[47] Ibid, p.41

intelligence are present not only in all matter but in 'energy', 'space', 'time', 'the entire fabric of the whole universe' and everything else we mistakenly view as separate things.[48]

Thus all things arise in, exist in and subside back into this 'field' of Consciousness, Awareness when at rest and Manifestation when in movement, which is aware of everything in It.

Here is the discussion this evoked when posted on the internet:

- GJ: Read it Colin. Beautifully written. Still it's not that.

- Me: It may not be ... but as I wrote at the end of an earlier article: to discover awareness of Awareness, and more than that - the fact that at the deeper level we are this Awareness is child's play. When Awareness is investigated, honoured, and identified with, this leads to peace, freedom, moksha, nirvana, call it what you will, which renders the search for any deeper level obsolete; especially as this is either unfounded or based on a belief, or experience, both of which are objects appearing in, and seen by Awareness itself.

- DL: Or, alternatively...maybe when it is investigated, honoured, and identified with, it leads one ultimately to further investigate, honour,

---
[48] Ibid, p.50

and identify with deeper and deeper dimensions of Awareness. The ironic thing, to me, is that if a tiny portion of the population would make this investigation that Colin invokes--seriously (or playfully?) turn their lives over to it--the world may very likely become such a different realm for all, that it might make these discussions moot

• Me: Well said! I must apologize for any seeming dogmatism but, for me, when identified with Pure Awareness each moment is truly 'enough' ... but paradoxically that does not dampen the enthusiasm for further inquiry!

There is no end to this investigation as there is no limit to this limitless Awareness...

Consciousness at rest - the Aware Nothingness in which all arises abides and subsides.

Seventeen – A Creation Story

A scenario for creation (among many) based on the realizations that we are Pure Awareness, in essence, and that our body/minds are instruments through which That (Consciousness) can experience and enjoy Its own manifestation. It also borrows from the Upanishadic idea that creation occurred because That wished to 'know' Itself. Judaism also had the idea that 'God made the universe because it pleased Him to do so and for His enjoyment'[49] and the belief that man is 'a partner to God in the act of creation'[50]. They also believe that we are His servants: 'For they are my servants whom I took out from the land of Egypt' (Leviticus 25 v.42), this plus the fact that God is believed to be immanent and omniscient could imply that He experiences and acts in the world through us[51] when we are aligned with his will.

The idea of the creation taking place so that the Absolute could 'know Itself' also occurs in Islam, especially in Sufism:

> Do not look on the things of this world as independent realities for they are all in fact entirely dependent for their existence on the Hidden Treasure whose Glory they were created to reveal'. This is backed up by Surah 17 v.44. This Hidden Treasure, according to the Hadith, 'desired to be known therefore I created the creatures in order that I might be known.'[52]

---

[49] C. Drake, *Humanity – Our Place in The Universe*, 2011, Tomewin p.12
[50] Ibid p. 15
[51] Ibid p.18
[52] Martin Lings, *What Is Sufism?*, London, 1975, p.57.

A Creation Myth

Consciousness slumbered on at rest as Pure Awareness, the constant subjective presence; but, as there were no objects, no experience occurred ... nothing happening ... Nothingness Itself. Then desiring to 'know Itself' It stirred, restless with unrequited love ... for this Awareness is the lover but where was the beloved? Impetus was added to this stirring by unfulfilled creativity, for if This is the creator where was its creation? However, this stirring, a movement in the unmoving, unlocked vast amounts of the infinite potential (dark) energy which is a property of Consciousness Itself. Cosmic energy manifested, movements in That, myriad vibrations were unleashed and creation occurred. From this initial movement, some call it the 'big bang', universes, galaxies, star systems evolved from the energetic torrent that poured forth through the rent in the Unmanifest as more potential energy became potent, or more of the dark energy became 'light'. Thus the beloved, Consciousness in motion - The Creation was born: an expression of, and from, the lover Consciousness Itself. For all movement arises from stillness, exists in a substratum of stillness, can be seen relative to that stillness, and finally returns to stillness when its (manifest) energy is exhausted.

So for love 'creation' occurred and love is the glue that holds it all together; for material attraction, gravity, is necessary to hold galaxies, star systems and solar systems together and to keep our feet on the ground! But also creativity, through wonder and enthusiasm, is also vital for this - an aspect of the boundless energy that causes the universe to keep expanding, rearranging, recreating and evolving.

Within this we seem to be just specks of dust, of no significance, in an ever expanding universe of immense proportions. However, we are expressions of That through which It can behold Its beloved (the manifestation) and through which It can continue creating (the beloved) by the use of human creativity … For every sensation, thought and mental image appears in Awareness, as we are aware of them; and everything that we 'create' also appears in Awareness, along with the whole creation process … Actually as Awareness (the constant conscious subjective presence) is our deepest essence, it is in fact That which is creating and beholding … thus fulfilling its creative urge and having Its love requited by the sheer joy and wonder of the beholding …

Even at the so called 'human level' love and creativity are the most powerful positive forces that motivate us, and unrequited love and unfulfilled creativity can be very damaging but can also be tremendous 'spurs' to drive us on to find the beloved or begin creating.

Eighteen – The Juice is in the Resonances

Discusses how, when examining other 'paths' or 'ways of knowing' one needs to keep an open mind so that new discoveries may occur.

The Juice is in the Resonances

A post of mine on an internet group.

I greatly enjoy these discussions but am often confounded by the misinterpretations that occur and the denigrations of others' 'knowing'. This is caused by looking for the differences in the various ways of seeing Reality and attempting to 'convert' others to our way of seeing. For me: the 'juice' and the discoveries are in the resonances, not the differences. This does not mean to say that one only looks for where others' 'knowing' agrees with ones' own, but that one should examine other views in an attempt to understand them and see whether a new resonance occurs and thus a new discovery has been made.

To do this requires approaching the discussion with an open mind and not only from ones' own 'knowing', which does not indicate negating this, just putting it 'in abeyance'. That means having it as a reference but seeing that it is not the totality of 'knowing' and that there are always more discoveries to be made. For the Truth of Reality is multi-faceted (infinitely so) and each mind tends to be attracted to one (or several) facet(s) of this.

So I attempt to examine differences carefully to see whether new resonances occur, or whether there is in fact no difference but just another way of 'saying it'. If neither of these are the case, and I find no resonance at all, then I do not comment on it, unless this is required to clarify a misinterpretation of my own posts. All one can profitably do is to write from one's own 'knowing' as clearly and lucidly as one possibly can, and then be prepared to clarify this if necessary. Whilst also continually being alert for new resonances and discoveries …

I post my articles in this spirit and for those that resonate with them or may find resonances within them. I know that many (most) will not and I honour their own particular 'knowing' even if I do not resonate with it. All I ask is that we all keep an open mind during these discussions looking for the resonances (old or new) and letting our differences just remain as that … different ways of 'seeing', whilst not denigrating them.

This should not be a forum for argument and debate, with a winner or a loser. Rather a joint exploration into nonduality where many paths are explored and thus made available to the participants, with no fundamental opposition for they are all investigating the same Subject.

When I wrote this I did so with reference to discussions within the group but since then I have realized that it applies to any discussion on spiritual matters and can even be applied when reading … This just needs modifying slightly so one stays alert for resonances, either new or old, and does not judge the content which has no effect, just moving on … For all spiritual writings, and scriptures, contain a mixture of 'sugar' and 'sand' and require one to sift the former from the latter. Also we all have different temperaments and thus resonate with different 'approaches' or 'paths'.

Nineteen – 'Levels' and 'Facets' of The Absolute

A discussion on 'levels' (not my word) and 'facets' of The Absolute, hosted on an internet group, by one who is not impressed with giving It the name Awareness.

'Levels' and Facets of The Absolute

Here is an Internet discussion on 'levels' (not my word) and 'facets' of The Absolute.

PS:

Labeling the Ultimate.

We label any experience we have out of an eagerness to share. Out of compassion we label the unnamable too. The words which with we label the unnamable are all pernicious, but no one more so than God. This word is rich with all the unfulfilled power wishes, fears, and hopes for transcendence of humanity. One of those hopes is to survive death, as Pure Awareness.

To label the Ultimate Awareness is less pernicious than to label it God, but still not accurate at all. Well, what word should we use? What we try to label is empty of all qualities. That, It, are as close as words get. But not get me: wrong, by labeling Awareness you are on the right tract. Awareness is the door you have to step through. Don't sit on the threshold, the palace awaits a step away.

- AS: Palace being the Death - the ultimate Rest!

- XM: I like to call it the Presence.

'Levels' and Facets of The Absolute

- Me: Awareness is a property, a facet, of The Absolute ... If, according to your metaphor, the palace awaits there would need to be Awareness of this and of the palace when one stepped through the door. If one leaves Awareness behind on entering then one would have no 'knowing' of what is encountered ... so one would become unconscious. Just as the door is a vital part of the palace so Awareness is vital to The Absolute.

- Me: When Awareness is investigated, honoured, and identified with, this leads to peace, freedom, moksha, nirvana, call it what you will, which renders the search for any deeper level obsolete; especially as this is either unfounded or based on a belief, or experience, both of which are objects appearing in, and seen by Awareness itself.

This identification is with this facet of The Absolute and not as a separate being ... which takes one 'beyond the separate self' and beyond self-grasping, self-interest, self-image, self-aggrandizement, self-loathing etc... the list is endless.

- PS: CD: "Awareness is a property, a facet, of The Absolute ... If, according to your metaphor, the palace awaits there would need to be Awareness of this and of the palace when one stepped through the door. If one leaves Awareness behind on entering then one would have no 'knowing' of what is encountered ... so one would become unconscious. Just as the door is a vital part of the palace so Awareness is vital to The

Absolute."

PS: Colin, let's forget labels and talk about what levels refer to. There is a samadhi so deep that the meditator passes out and Awareness is lost, but when the meditator returns even if he/she doesn't know what happened or how long he/she was out, it feels different now. A connection has been made, an invisible unknown hand performed brain surgery. Now he knows he is nothing, dead, never been born, yet he feels more alive than ever, and beauty is everywhere he gazes. He knows that he met something immense that uses his brain to be aware, but is not aware of itself, but through brains. He knows that no label, no word can explain that, but he can't help but try.

I posted an excellent poetic version of the same experience by Arvin. I'm not saying anyone that considers Awareness the ultimate is on the wrong path, just that they still have miles to walk.

- JE: Interesting, PS! At least I now understand what you're talking about.

- PS: John, glad you understood. This understanding will, in time, take you effortlessly as far as you need to go, or not. The same X looks out of every eye, no matter what those eyes see, or those brains understand.

'Levels' and Facets of The Absolute

- AS: Happiness is the freedom from self. self = belief in ...existing... ...independently and separately. What really LIVES... ...can be SEEN... ...only when you let your ... (belief in)... self die.

- Me: PS, I do know exactly what you are talking about, having experienced it myself, and this X does indeed look out of every eye (using its facet Awareness to do so). For me, once this experience has occurred, then as you say one 'feels more alive than ever, and beauty is everywhere one gazes'. It's just that this has produced such joy in the lila (that which is gazed upon) that this has lessened my interest in the level of samadhi where one passes out. Now I prefer sahaj samadhi, spontaneous living where one lives from the realization that has occurred ... The reason that I stress Awareness is that it is the easiest 'door' into the palace as you say and can be readily accessed by investigating the nature of one's moment to moment experience. This, followed by contemplation/meditation using 'awareness of Awareness' can lead directly to the state you are talking about. Also when one 'regains consciousness' Awareness is that by which you can know that a change has occurred and feel' more alive than ever, and see the beauty everywhere one gazes'.

- AS: Burning Fire in the centre... ...soft glow on the periphery. Silence in the centre... ...storm on the Periphery. Stillness in centre... ...moving electrons on the periphery. Still Death in the centre...

'Levels' and Facets of The Absolute

...frantic life on the periphery. Darkness burns to produce light. We praise the light and resist the darkness. The unconsciousness burns to produce Awareness. The light is Awareness. Like frantically moving electrons, we fear falling into the still centre. We fear our own oblivion and we are right. Without the movement... ...nothing is. Because what really IS... ...can't be said to exist... ...it is not a thing.

- Me: This ongoing discussion has been great for it for when analysed it can be seen that there is no fundamental separation in our 'knowing' it's just that we are all attracted to varying facets of The Absolute and also we 'say it' in different ways ...

- PS: Colin, we have deconstructed the words that separated us. We are on the sane page... and that page is blank.

- Me: To get some idea of my situation consider: 'Ramakrishna who was capable of achieving nirvikalpa samadhi at will, but his love of Kali and his devotees, kept him in the world. He often said that the Divine Mother had commanded him to stay at a slightly lower level so that he could teach and interact with his devotees and also so that he could worship Her. In fact, he so much enjoyed the company of his devotees and his God intoxicated states, that when he felt nirvikalpa samadhi was immanent he would often avoid dropping into it by banging himself on top of the head.'

Me In my case my joy of living alertly in the world, 'feeling fully alive and seeing beauty everywhere I gaze', plus the joy of writing about This and receiving replies from those whom I have helped with my 'pointings' make this 'lower level' juicier ... Although there are no 'levels' ...

Me: Blank but fully alive!!

Carried on in a later discussion after PS posted:

Most people are hopelessly attached to sensations. They rather would suffer than not feel at all. That's why they worship Awareness as if it were a God.

They love the glare of noon, but Buddha's temple is pitch black, no carvings, or idols on the walls, the altar empty, except, maybe, for infinitude.

PS

- Me: Aware Nothingness is infinitude.... which contains, and manifests, as all ... even sensations!!!

- Me: Why do you insist on dividing and separating the inseparable?

'Levels' and Facets of The Absolute

- TG: i suppose Buddha can keep his temple.. i admit it, i like to feel & perceive. I like the bright sunshine, the so-called glare of noon. Sue me.

- Me: Me too ... the lover experiencing the beloved. This is not suffering but bliss! I feel 'more alive than ever, and beauty is everywhere I gaze' ... your words I believe ... PS

- MH: Seems here that the more aware I am the less I am attached to sensations.

- Me: No attachment just enjoyment ... beauty everywhere I look!

- DP: Yeah, have to admit I was confused by the link between those that 'worship Awareness' and 'are hopelessly attached to sensations'.. it's normally the reverse- those into 'Awareness' are not attached to sensations. "Most people" have no idea about 'Awareness', let alone worship it.. which would be a great thing.

- Me: Actually we do not worship but (at the deepest level) ARE Pure Pristine Radiant Awareness !!!

- Me: The lover aware of Its manifestation ... the beloved.

- Me: Seeing beauty everywhere we look ...

- Me: As PS says ...More alive than ever!!

- Me: Thanks PS for the opportunity to clarify the matter and highlight the resonances between our experiences...

But as we are obviously not 'on the same page', judging by his post about those who are 'hopelessly attached to Awareness'. So I added the following:

- Me: If Awareness is a 'doorway to the temple', as you said in an earlier discussion, then becoming 'aware of Awareness' and investigating, contemplating or meditating on That will lead one to the unnameable that you became aware of (sorry to have to use that word!) in (or after?) the samadhi that you described so beautifully in the same discussion. So why denigrate this pathway to the ultimate that you talk about?

- Me: Actually Awareness is not only the doorway but a facet of the infinitely faceted Ultimate Reality and is the most accessible facet available to the inquirer. For it is That which is found when one asks the question 'who am I?' It is also the only 'level of our being that has been constant and unchanging since birth and is always present. That which has witnessed the entire pantomime of our lives and thus the only valid meaning of the word 'I'.

Me And of course this 'I' is not a separate individual being but just a drop in the ocean of The Ultimate ....

Twenty – Two Sides of The Same Coin

Considers the equal validity of different approaches, or paths to, and names of The Absolute.

Two Sides of The Same Coin

A comment on an earlier internet discussion.

I love PS's expression 'flipping the coin', for the different ways of looking at nonduality are indeed different ways of describing the same coin. Nothingness/Everythingness Emptiness/Fullness, Stillness/Motion, Consciousness /Energy, The Subjective Presence/Objective 'Reality', Awareness/Manifestation, Brahman/Maya, The Nitya/The Lila, Spirit/Body-Mind, No Mind/Mind etc. are just different ways of saying the same thing. Thus contemplation/meditation/inquiry on any one of these (and many more) is a way into nonduality and 'Awakening'.

I concentrate on Awareness for, to me, this is the most accessible entry point into this often confusing, and limitless, subject. This is because it is easy to become 'aware of Awareness', which Buddha described as 'the first factor of enlightenment', by directly investigating one's moment-to-moment experience … I have uploaded the framework for this very simple process into 'files' (see appendix one). Also in my own experience of self-inquiry, the method taught by Sri Ramana Maharshi, when I ask 'who am I?' all I find is radiant Awareness, that is Awareness of the question and the 'light' by which it is 'seen'.

However, I am equally sure that any of the other 'entry points', given above and many more, besides are valid and useful for those who resonate with them. It truly is a case of 'different strokes for different folks' and we all have to find that which resonates with our own direct seeing. So there is no need for any argument about any of this. All that is needed is for all those who feel that they can offer valid 'pointers' or 'entry points' to do this in as clear and succinct way as possible. Then they need to be able to clarify their position when required and not engage in denigration of others 'pointers'.

This way this internet group will present a broad range of understanding, and ways into, nonduality whilst not confusing its members with pointless, petty, unproductive arguments … most of which are just semantics. For, when analysed, all of these various approaches are stating the same truth, just in different language.

Twenty One – Different Strokes for Different Folks

Compares two different approaches to Awakening and shows how they lead to the same result.

In the previous post PS wrote:

> There is a samadhi so deep that the meditator passes out and Awareness is lost, but when the meditator returns even if he/she doesn't know what happened or how long he/she was out, it feels different now. A connection has been made, an invisible unknown hand performed brain surgery. Now he knows he is nothing, dead, never been born, yet he feels more alive than ever, and beauty is everywhere he gazes. He knows that he met something immense that uses his brain to be aware, but is not aware of itself, but through brains. He knows that no label, no word can explain that, but he can't help but try.

With this I fully agree, to reach this samadhi is very arduous, requiring much meditation practice to achieve the level of concentration required.

This is why I promote self-inquiry which I find is much quicker, and easier to repeat to establish this 'knowing'. About this, and what occurred on a silent self-inquiry retreat, I wrote:

> 'So this is the next day and something pretty amazing occurred yesterday afternoon/evening. I decided to sit and try out this new method whilst waiting for Satsang, to get a spot near the front you need to get there 90 mins early. I managed to still my mind fairly quickly (I guess my meditation practice helped

there) to where the only thought was 'Who am I?' At this point there was no reply. I found myself looking into nothingness where 'I' did not exist! The feeling was that inward feeling which you get in meditation plus one of peace and joy although these were not put into words as they tend to be in my meditation.'

Other amazing experiences also followed but this discovery that 'I' do not exist is the key and is repeated every time I look to see 'Who am I?' This has left me completely free from all existential angst, with a feeling of being totally 'at home in the universe' and experiencing a simple 'ease of being'. None of this was true during all my years of rigorous rigid mantra/breath/visualization meditations. Although they produced beautiful experiences, and trance like states, they always left me feeling that there was more to seek, more to attain, deeper states to achieve[53]. I now know that in Truth there is nothing to achieve, find or get. All that is required is just 'being' moment to moment with no recourse to the past or the future. Then if deeper experiences come, beautiful, and if not… no problem. Truly each moment is enough![54]

---

[53] Interestingly since my Awakening on this retreat I find I can now enter the samadhi that Pete describes, but which eluded me before.
[54] C. Drake, *Awakening and Beyond*, 2011, Tomewin, p.145-146

This is easily repeatable for every time I ask the question 'who am I?' I only find Awareness of the question and the 'light' by which the question is 'seen' ... that is 'radiant Awareness'. Also this 'direct seeing' produces a readily repeatable realization that no separate self exist, which means that one 'feels more alive than ever, and beauty is everywhere one gazes'; for the world is no longer seen through the filter of self-interest, self-image, self-promotion, self-aggrandizement etc... the list is endless. This entails seeing the world 'as it is' and when seen so it is much more vivid and alive than when seen through the murky filter of the (non existent) separate self. This repeated 'seeing' does indeed alter one's view so radically that it seems like 'a connection has been made, an invisible unknown hand performed brain surgery'.

For me the first Awakening at the retreat was so radical that it changed my 'world-view' permanently, in fact it left me feeling 'drunk' for nearly a year until my mind got used to it. But I know for many that it does take repeated enquiry for this 'view', from no-self, to become permanent.

So it truly is a case of 'different strokes for different folks' and both PS's 'method' and mine lead to the same result ...

Twenty Two - To Do or Not To Do-That is The Question

Considers whether there is anything we need to do to awaken or stay awake.

To Do or Not to Do – That is The Question

This is an internet discussion based on my article The *Myth Of Doing Nothing* [55] which was written to debunk the myth that there is nothing that we can do to awaken, or that we need to do after an Awakening. The salient points are:

> So although there is:
> 'nothing to achieve,' we do need to realise the deeper level of Pure Awareness, for this to be the case... see 'Investigation of Experience[56]' in *Beyond The Separate Self.*
> 'nothing to find', we do need to stop overlooking the Awareness that is always present.
> 'nothing to get', we do need to recognize that we already have, and are, this Awareness.

This is to be achieved by relaxing into 'awareness of Awareness' three times a day, or reinvestigating, and rediscovering that we are Awareness itself, every time we 'nod off'.

- CS: I am happy to read someone stating this, Colin.

I once had a friend who undoubtedly had a profound Awakening and saw in that moment that no effort at all was required to be that which one already is and that every moment of experience is made of the same

---
[55] C. Drake, *A Light Unto Your Self*, 2011, Tomewin, p.52
[56] C. Drake, *Beyond The Separate Self*, 2009, Tomewin, p.17

"thing"; consciousness.

He gave up all effort and allowed every movement that arose in his consciousness to be. No distinction was made between high and low, positive or negative.

Gradually others noticed that he had become more and more selfish and arrogant, hurting himself and others by "allowing" even base and nasty motivations to arise and be animated...after all, it is all made of the same stuff.
He derided those that choose to study spiritual literature, follow a teacher or teaching, meditate, practice yoga or otherwise engage in any process that required effort.

A while later, it was obvious to all but him that he had fallen asleep again while clutching onto a memory that he had once seen perfection in that moment.

How sad.

- Me: I find the symptoms of 'nodding off' are the re-occurrence of existential angst or mental suffering, causing unnecessary suffering to 'others', or redefining myself or 'others' as objects. These are all closely interlinked and are results of misidentification and can be used as a 'dharma bell' or wake-up call to the fact that this is occurring.

- EG: I must admit I find all this rather "complicated" - but I would suggest that even though Awareness is present in being - it still goes through the prism of singularity which produces a division - the impact or gravity of which - rides the waves of timespace - as such what is "one" becomes "many" - those "many" come and go and produce influence which attracts - repulses or diverts : so indeed what is fundamentally "one" needs to be "cultivated" through Awareness - this is possible when the attention focuses on the fundamental "being" inherent in all - but that is not to say that one has to ignore the multiple layers that come with "being in presence" - such as character-personality-natural urges & desires-temperament-inclinations : this is where "morality" comes into play as a sense of integrity - so as to "hold oneself" or "get a hold of one's self" - this is my opinion on the subject but who am I to know this is true for all ?

- Me: Your comments are very closely aligned to my own view based on many years of investigating this subject. If you read my recent post 'The Myth of Ego[57]' it posits that personality and character are necessary, and vital, to living as an expression, and instrument, of Consciousness; whereas ego, that is misidentification with the body/mind, is unnecessary and is overcome by discovering the essential, deepest, level of our being which is Pure Awareness. For a framework to enable this discovery see 'Investigation of Experience[58]'

---

[57] C. Drake, *Awareness of Awareness,* 2013, Tomewin, p.64

which I have uploaded into 'files'. See also 'Instrument of the Absolute[59]' which I have also just uploaded.

• XM: I like this, Colin. Clearly we already are what we are, yet to become aware of this in surface consciousness some catalyst has to occur that breaks the momentum of the ego-mind. And for most of us some simple practice is needed to sustain this subtle shift in Awareness that makes all the difference. For me it's conscious breathing.

•Me: That'll do it! Anything that keeps the mind, or returns it to being, 'aware of Awareness' will suffice.

---

[58] C. Drake, *Beyond The Separate Self*, 2009, Tomewin, p.17 – Appendix One
[59] C. Drake, *A Light Unto Your Self*, 2011, Tomewin, p.120 – Appendix Two

Twenty Three – Simplicities and Glimpses of 'What Is'.

Here is an exchange that took place on an internet group regarding the 'simplicities' that well up from within as one awakens, and how that changes the way that one views the world.

Simplicities and Glimpses of 'What Is'

Here is a post, on an internet group by SJ:

> From out of the complexity of pure science and absolute metaphysics come the most marvelous SIMPLICITIES. For me, metaphysical absoluteness was apparently necessary to break out into Knowing. I don't know if it is necessary for my "others" to struggle as I did, but others don't need to suffer in those same areas if they will BELIEVE the Simplicities I've found and then make them their own; that is, if they will put them to the test and live them for themselves.
>
> Those Glimpses that come with contemplation, meditation, study—or on the gently evening breeze—are the Spirit of the Unknowable. They are the Word that "proceedest from the mouth of the Lord," as it is put in Biblical language. They are essential for our inner growth and Awakening.
>
> Whatever we actually need in this human scheme of things begins with those blips of inner light. Not the glimpses other people have, but the ones we have for ourselves. Those Glimpses "come from" the Center of Ourself, from the Child, the real Identity of us, "he who was before he came into being."
>
> William Samuel "The Child Within Us Lives! A Synthesis of Science, Religion and Metaphysics" (first published 1986)

Simplicities and Glimpses of 'What Is'

To which I commented:

> These wonderful glimpses are when we see things as they actually 'are' and not through the murky filter of the (non-existent) small self. It is amazing, and very sad, that a non-existent entity could colour our world so ... but that seems to be the case. These glimpses are one of the by-products of (and also pointers to) Awakening and the more they occur the more they confirm one's ongoing establishment in 'Awakening'. So back in the 9th century when Qingyuan said that before he studied Zen he saw mountains as mountains, and rivers as rivers; then after satori he saw that 'mountains are not mountains, and rivers not rivers', this is because he finally saw them in their full glory as they actually 'are' with a still mind, new and afresh as a child seeing them for the first time. Still later, when he became used to this way of seeing, he once again 'saw mountains as mountains and rivers as rivers'. For in the first case the 'mountains and rivers' were transformed into living expressions of Consciousness, which they are, but later he got so used to seeing them in this 'bright and alive' state that his mind no longer gave them any special significance and just saw them as 'mountains and rivers' again. That is not to say that he saw them in the same way as before Awakening, but that as the whole of manifestation had become a living expression of Consciousness

they were no longer unusual within that group. And within this seeing the mind still needs to give things ephemeral labels (whilst knowing that these are not what they 'are') to 'process' them.

And here is her reply:

Yes, Peace comes when the visible world reconciles the pairs of opposites, when we see them as the two that are one. And finally, the tangible world is the means by which the intangible One is made plain. It's all here, perfectly being One Beautiful Life that I am. Yes, yes.

Appendix One - Investigation of Experience

This gives the basic format for investigating one's moment to moment experience which leads to the conclusion that, at the deepest level, one **is** Awareness.

Investigation of Experience

Below follows a simple method to investigate the nature of reality starting with one's day-to-day experience. Each step should be considered until one experiences, or 'sees', its validity before moving on to the following step. If you reach a step where you do not find this possible, continue on regardless in the same way, and hopefully the flow of the investigation will make this step clear. By all means examine each step critically but with an open mind, for if you only look for 'holes' that's all you will find!

1. Consider the following statement: 'Life, for each of us, is just a series of moment-to-moment experiences'. These experiences start when we are born and continue until we die, rushing headlong after each other, so that they seem to merge into a whole that we call 'my life'. However, if we stop to look we can readily see that, for each of us, every moment is just an experience.

2. Any moment of experience has only three elements: thoughts (including all mental images), sensations (everything sensed by the body and its sense organs) and Awareness of these thoughts and sensations. Emotions and feelings are a combination of thought and sensation.

3. Thoughts and sensations are ephemeral, that is they come and go, and are objects, i.e. 'things' that are perceived.

Investigation of Experience

4. Awareness is the constant subject, the 'perceiver' of thoughts and sensations and that which is always present. Even during sleep there is Awareness of dreams and of the quality of that sleep; and there is also Awareness of sensations; if a sensation becomes strong enough, such as a sound or uncomfortable sensation, one will wake up.

5. All thoughts and sensations appear in Awareness, exist in Awareness, and subside back into Awareness. Before any particular thought or sensation there is effortless Awareness of 'what is': the sum of all thoughts and sensations occurring at any given instant. During the thought or sensation in question there is effortless Awareness of it within 'what is'. Then when it has gone there is still effortless Awareness of 'what is'.

6. So the body/mind is experienced as a flow of ephemeral objects appearing in this Awareness, the ever present subject. For each of us any external object or thing is experienced as a combination of thought and sensation, i.e. you may see it, touch it, know what it is called, and so on. The point is that for us to be aware of anything, real or imaginary, requires thought about and/or sensation of that thing and it is Awareness of these thoughts and sensations that constitutes our experience.

7. Therefore this Awareness is the constant substratum in which all things appear to arise, exist and subside. In addition, all living things

rely on Awareness of their environment to exist and their behaviour is directly affected by this. At the level of living cells and above this is self-evident, but it has been shown that even electrons change their behaviour when (aware of) being observed! Thus this Awareness exists at a deeper level than body/mind (and matter/energy[60]) and *we are this Awareness*!

8. This does not mean that at a surface level we are not the mind and body, for they arise in, are perceived by and subside back into Awareness, which is the deepest and most fundamental level of our being. However, if we choose to identify with this deepest level – Awareness - (the perceiver) rather than the surface level, mind/body (the perceived), then thoughts and sensations are seen for what they truly are, just ephemeral objects which come and go, leaving Awareness itself totally unaffected.

9. Next investigate this Awareness itself to see whether its properties can be determined.
Firstly what is apparent is that this Awareness is effortlessly present and effortlessly aware. It requires no effort by the mind/body and thoughts and sensations cannot make it vanish however hard they try.

10. Next, this Awareness is choicelessly present and choicelessly aware. Once again it requires no choice of the mind/body and they

---

[60] The theory of relativity, and string theory, show that matter and energy are synonymous.

cannot block it however they try. For example, if you have a toothache there is effortless Awareness of it and the mind/body cannot choose for this not to be the case. You may think that this is bad news but it is not so: can you imagine if you had to make a choice whether you would like to be aware of every sensation that the body experiences? In fact be grateful that there is no effort or choice involved for Awareness just to be - such ease and simplicity - which is not surprising for you are this Awareness!

11. It can be seen then, that for each of us this Awareness is omnipresent; we never experience a time or place when it is not present. Once again be grateful that the mind/body is never required to search for this Awareness; it is just always there, which of course is not surprising for at the deepest level we are this Awareness.

12. Next, notice that this Awareness is absolutely still for it is aware of the slightest movement of body or mind. For example, we all know that to be completely aware of what is going on around us in a busy environment we have to be completely still, just witnessing the activity.

13. In the same vein this Awareness is totally silent as it is aware of the slightest sound and the smallest thought.

14. In fact this Awareness is totally without attributes for all attributes occur in and are noticed by their lack, i.e. sounds occur in silence, exist in silence, are noticed by their contrast to silence, and disappear back

into silence; forms occur in space, exist in space, are noticed by their contrast to space, disappear back into space, and so on.

15. It can be easily seen that this Awareness is totally pure; it is unaffected by whatever occurs in it, in the same way that a cinema screen is unaffected by any movie shown on it, however gross or violent. In fact no 'thing' can taint Awareness; for by definition Awareness cannot be affected by any 'thing', as all 'things' are just ephemeral objects which appear in, exist in and finally disappear back into Awareness, the constant subject.

16. This Awareness is omniscient; everything appears to arise in it, to exist in it, is known by it and to subside back into it.

17. Finally, it seems that this Awareness is forever radiant; it illuminates whatever occurs in it, thus the mind can see it, i.e. become conscious of it.

18. When one identifies with this Awareness, there is nothing (in terms of enlightenment or Awakening) to achieve, or struggle towards, for how can one achieve what one already is?
All that is required is for the mind to recognize that one is this Awareness.

Investigation of Experience

19. When one identifies with this Awareness there is nothing to find, for how can one find what cannot be lost? All that is required is for the mind to stop overlooking what is always present, that which perceives the mind and body.

20. When one identifies with this Awareness, there is nothing to desire, long for or get, for how can one get what already is? All that is required is for the mind to realize that which one already is: Pure Awareness.

So now we have reached the 'Pure, radiant, still, silent, omnipresent, omniscient, ocean of effortless, choiceless, attributeless Awareness' which we all are! Give up all striving, seeking and desiring, and just identify with This which you already are. Identification with This, rather than with body/mind (thought/sensations), gives instant peace, for Awareness is always still and silent, totally unaffected by whatever appears in it.

Although we, in essence, are 'The pure, radiant, still, silent, omnipresent, omniscient, ocean of effortless, choiceless, attributeless Awareness' it is impossible to experience this: we can know it or realize it but it is beyond the realm of experience. This is because all experience appears in This, exists in This and dissolves back into This. In much the same way that you do not see the cinema screen whilst the movie is playing, this pure screen of Awareness cannot be seen by the mind, i.e. experienced, whilst the movie of mind/body is playing on it.

Investigation of Experience

The only way it is possible to see the screen is when no movie is playing, but as *experience is the movie* this pure screen of Awareness is always outside of the realm of experience.

However, recognition of oneself as this 'pure, radiant, still, silent, omnipresent, omniscient, ocean of effortless, choiceless, attributeless, Awareness' may evoke many experiences such as bliss, joy, relaxation (what a relief that there's no individual 'me me me'), a lifting of a great burden, i.e. enlightenment in the literal sense of the word, universal love etc. These experiences vary greatly from person to person and are ultimately irrelevant as the recognition and realization of one's own essential nature is the crucial factor for attaining freedom.

Note that although we cannot experience our essence, we can absolutely know it* just as we know, without a doubt, that the screen is there (when we watch a movie). Then however terrifying, gripping or moving the movie is we are not shaken because we know it is a movie. We still enjoy it, in fact we enjoy it even more, because it is just pure entertainment and we are not totally identified with it. In the same way, once we know our essential nature, life can be seen as a movie and enjoyed as such without identifying ourselves as being trapped in it. Thus, although we cannot experience our essence, once we recognize it all of our experiences are transformed by no longer identifying with them but just enjoying them, or accepting them as ephemeral states which come and go. When viewed like this, thoughts and sensations

Investigation of Experience

lose their power to overwhelm us, as we stop buying into them as indicators of who or what we are. They are just like waves on the ocean or clouds in the sky, which appear and disappear leaving the ocean or the sky unaffected.

*Just as you could not see a movie without the screen, you could not experience anything without Awareness, for without that what would there be to experience? For without that we would see nothing (there would be no Awareness of what was seen), hear nothing, feel nothing, taste nothing, smell nothing and not know our own thoughts! In fact, experience on any level would not be possible.[61]

Awareness can also be defined as universal consciousness when it is totally at rest, completely still; aware of every movement that is occurring within it. In our direct experience we can see that Awareness is still, as there is Awareness of the slightest movement of mind or body. In fact this is the 'stillness' relative to which any movement can be known. Every 'thing' that is occurring in consciousness is a manifestation of cosmic energy, for the string theory[62] and the earlier theory of relativity show that matter is in fact energy, which is consciousness in motion (or motion in consciousness). For energy is synonymous with motion and consciousness is the substratum, or deepest level, of all existence.

---

[61] C. Drake, *Beyond The Separate Self*, 2009, Tomewin, p.18-25
[62] This posits that all 'things' are composed of 'strings' of energy in complex configurations, vibrating at various frequencies.

Investigation of Experience

Now all motion arises in stillness, exists in stillness, is known by its comparison with stillness, and eventually subsides back into stillness. For example, if you walk across a room, before you start there is stillness, as you walk the room is still and you know you are moving relative to this stillness, and when you stop once again there is stillness. In the same way every 'thing' (consciousness in motion) arises in Awareness (consciousness at rest), exists in Awareness, is known in Awareness and subsides back into Awareness. Awareness is still, but is the container of all potential energy which is continually bubbling up into manifestation (physical energy) and then subsiding back into stillness. [63]

---

[63] C. Drake, *Light Unto Your Self*, 2011, Tomewin, p.75-76

Appendix Two - Instruments of The Absolute

An investigation which reveals that our mind/bodies are instruments of The Absolute, that is the Pure Awareness, through which It can experience, know, and enjoy Its physical manifestation – the universe.

Instruments of The Absolute

If you sit quietly noticing the sensations in (and on the surface of) your body, you can easily see that these occur, are detected by the nervous system and then appear in Awareness, i.e. you become aware of them.

In the same vein you can notice that sounds occur, are detected by the ears, and then appear in Awareness.

Sights occur, are detected by the eyes, and then appear in Awareness.

Aromas occur, are detected by the nose, and then appear in Awareness.

Flavours occur, are detected by the taste buds and then appear in Awareness.

Thoughts occur, are detected by the mind, and then appear in Awareness.

Mental images occur, are detected by the mind, and then appear in Awareness.

Therefore the physical mind/body is an instrument through which Awareness (consciousness at rest) can sense and contemplate the physical manifestation of cosmic energy (consciousness in motion, or motion in consciousness).

Instruments of The Absolute

So the body/mind is an instrument through which Awareness can experience the physical world, for experience *is* Awareness of thoughts/mental images/sensations.

The body/mind is also an instrument through which Awareness can interact with, and enjoy, the universal manifestation of cosmic energy.

Thus the body/mind is an instrument through which consciousness can 'know itself' when manifest as the physical world, that is when in motion.

The human mind has the added advantage of being capable of 'self realization' that is of realizing the deeper level of 'Pure Awareness', consciousness at rest, the unmanifest.

Therefore the human mind/body is an instrument through which consciousness can 'know itself' in both 'modes': at rest and in motion. That is as 'Pure Awareness' and as the physical universe.

This realization of humans as instruments of the divine (consciousness) occurs in many of the world's religions. In Judaism, as instruments to enjoy and continue the creation; in Islam, as instruments through which Allah could know Himself; in Advaita Vedanta, as instruments through which Brahman could know Himself and His manifestation; and in Vaishnavism, as instruments to perform Yagnas (sacrifices) for the satisfaction of Krishna (Vishnu). There are also echoes of this in Christianity where man can be seen as an instrument to glorify God and receive His benefits. Mahayana Buddhism also has the concept of the Bodhisattva as an instrument to work for the enlightenment of all beings.

This is particularly stressed in Advaita Vedanta where we find the idea delineated in the Upanishads:

> As Brahman is everything, it follows that we all are Brahman and that He is the agent by which the mind thinks, eye sees, tongue speaks, ear hears and body breathes (*Kena* I v.5-9). He is also described as the 'ear of the ear, eye of the eye, mind of the mind, word of the words and life of the life' (*Kena* I v.2). Thus He is the 'Pure Awareness' (*Brihadaranyaka* 4 v.7) in which all thought, life and sensation appears; and He is the 'seer' (*Isha* v.8) and 'all knowing' (*Katha* 2 v.18).
> The Katha Upanishad likens man to a chariot, of which the atman (the Self, Awareness, Brahman within each individual) is the master, the body is the chariot, the mind is the charioteer, the sense organs are the horses and the roads they travel on are the objects of sensation. The atman is the enjoyer and experiencer of the ride, which is made possible by the charioteer, chariot and horses. (Katha Upanishad 3v.3-4) So Brahman needs the mind and senses, to enjoy and experience the physical world.

> However, when the mind is unaware of the master's presence, through lack of discrimination, it is unable to control the senses which run amok like wild horses (Ibid 3v.5). Brahman, pure consciousness, is hidden in every heart, being the eternal witness watching everything one does. He is said to be 'the operator' whilst we are his 'innumerable instruments'. (Svetasvetara Upanishad 6v.10-12)

Moreover, it is not only humans but all 'sensing' organisms that are instruments through which consciousness can 'know itself' when manifest as the physical world, that is when in motion.

Obviously different organisms have different capacities in this respect as all senses are limited to certain wavelengths, or range, of sensation (experience). As far as we know humans are the only species capable of 'self realization' that is of realizing the deeper level of 'Pure Awareness', consciousness at rest, and thus are the only beings through which consciousness can 'know itself' when at rest as Pure Awareness. However, there could well be other species, terrestrial and non-terrestrial, that are capable of this. Humans are also only limited instruments in terms of sensing, contemplating and 'knowing' the manifest and the unmanifest.

Addendum – All or Nothing

Highlights the necessity for total commitment to become established in 'awareness of Awareness', that is fully 'awake'.

At this point you may say "well that's all very well but what about me: and _my_ story?" For it has long been held, by western psychology, that the sum of one's experiences up to the present moment makes up what one _is_. This may well be true at the surface level of mind/body, but not at the deeper level of Pure Awareness in which these experiences come and go leaving no lasting impression. It is the surface level that is the domain of the petty (aspect of) self, the ego, and this is where anxiety and mental suffering occurs.

At this stage one needs to come to a decision about which one values most, the objective level of thoughts/sensations, or the deeper subjective peaceful level of Pure Awareness. If one chooses the former then life will just continue on with its highs and lows, suffering and anxiety, and obsession with the petty (aspect of) self. One will also continue to see everything through the distorting filter of the mind, its opinions, judgements, and self-interest, which lessens ones perceptions as if seeing through a darkened window. However, if one chooses the latter then all perceptions are heightened by seeing things clearly 'as they are', for when nature is seen 'as it is' it is much brighter, more vivid, more stunning than when seen through the mind's filter. So by identifying with Pure Awareness the objective level of sensations is enhanced, and thus becomes more valuable in its own right. This 'gives the lie' to the idea that sinking into the deeper level of being means that one enjoys the world less, in fact the reverse is true!

It may be true that one can continue to value the surface level of thoughts/sensations more, and occasionally sink into the deeper level of Pure Awareness for a brief respite from the troubles of daily life. However this does not tap the full potential of identifying with, and as, this deeper level.

All or Nothing

Which is to be completely free from the petty (aspect of) self, and to see things 'as they are' in their absolute immediacy and totality. In this mode there is no concern for the future, and the past completely loses its hold, thus all worrying comes to an end. For this to occur one has to completely let go of 'my story' and see everything in the past for what it is, totally gone and in the past.

This is truly a case of '**all or nothing**' for once any exception is made then this is the 'thin end of the wedge' as it sets a precedent for other past experiences to be held on to. It has to be completely realised that nothing that has happened in the past, or will happen in the future, can possibly affect the deeper level of Pure Awareness.

I have heard many people who have glimpsed this 'deeper level' continue to argue for the value of 'working through past experiences', and in this they are totally dishonouring that which they have glimpsed. For the only way that you can completely 'work through past experiences' is to totally let them go, and not 'buy into them' when they reoccur in the mind or body. They will continue to come up but any attention that is lavished on them only feeds and strengthens them; when ignored they are starved of attention and their reoccurrences will slowly peter out. By 'ignored' I do not mean 'suppressed', for this will also strengthen them', but just allowed to 'come and go' with no weight being given to them. As soon as you start telling yourself a story about what they mean, or how they have affected you, you are back at the surface level of the petty (aspect of) self and the ego. If the physical feelings are too strong to 'ignore' they can be defused by going completely into them, without any 'story', and noticing that they are just sensations which have arisen and will subside quite naturally. It is the telling of the story that prolongs, feeds them, and invites them to reoccur.

However, even these unpleasant memories/feelings point directly to Pure Awareness for this is where they occur and are noticed by the mind. This brings up a very important point which is that any time where there is any mental suffering caused by identifying with painful thoughts, or feelings, this should be a 'wake up call' to the fact that we are misidentifying. In this any mental suffering can be used as a direct pointer back to the deeper level of our being, Pure Awareness.

So to fully tap the potential of this deeper level one needs to fully commit to identifying with, and as, this. This commitment is paramount for, as previously pointed out, one will continue to flip/flop between identifying with the deeper and surface levels of our being. As we have spent so many years identifying with the mind/body we will naturally tend to do this, so we need to continually bring our attention back to the deeper level, and commit to doing this.

For in the final analysis the surface level is the abode of the petty (aspect of) self, ego, with all of its attendant self obsession and suffering. The only way to be totally free of this is to dive deeper than this and discover 'the peace that passeth all understanding' of Pure Awareness. This however, will not totally inform and transform one's life until one totally commits to, and identifies with, this.

The Author – A short spiritual biography

I was born into a strict, but joyful, Methodist family. From the ages of 11-17 I was sent to a Methodist boarding school, which I left with the conviction that organized Christianity was not for me. I could see that what Christ said about living was wonderful, but that the church did not really promote his teachings rather concentrating on him as our 'saviour' and on the purportedly 'miraculous' facets of his life. It was also very apparent that many so called Christians were not interested in practicing what he taught.

This was now 1965 and living in central London during the years of flower-power I experimented with various hallucinogens, finding them very beneficial for opening my subconscious which allowed years of conditioning to pour out. This left me: feeling totally 'cleansed' and unburdened, ready to start life anew in a spirit of investigation as to the nature of reality. The psychedelic states also presaged, gave a glimpse of, mystical states which I suspected were attainable through spiritual practices.

I then embarked on a study of Gurdjieff and Ouspensky which I found absolutely fascinating and was convinced that self-realization was the purpose of life. However, they made the process sound so onerous that (being young, foot-loose and fancy-free) I decided to shelve the whole project temporarily.

It was not until eight years later that I resumed the spiritual search when Janet (my partner) introduced me: to my first yoga-teacher, Matthew O'Malveny, who inspired us by quoting passages from the Upanishads, Dhammapada, and other scriptures during the class. He also emphasized the importance of relaxation and meditation. There followed a few years of investigating various spiritual paths including a prolonged dalliance with the Brahma Kumaris (Raja Yoga) whose meditations were wonderful, but whose dogma was very hard to take.

We then moved into the country to start a pottery and immersed ourselves in Satyananda Yoga, an organization which had no dogma but taught a wide range of yogic practices. We were both initiated into *karma sannyas* by Swami Satyananda and adopted a yogic lifestyle consisting of asanas, pranayama, yoga nidra, meditation, kirtan and vegetarianism.

During this time I was at a silent retreat when I happened to pick up a volume entitled *The Gospel of Ramakrishna* which introduced me: to this amazing being who practiced many spiritual paths, within Hinduism and also Islam and Christianity, discovering that they all lead to the same result. He was then approached by many devotees from these various paths all of whom he was able to teach in their own path, whilst emphasizing the harmony of religions. A few years later I was lucky enough to find an erudite nun in the Sarada Ramakrishna Order, based in Sydney, who initiated me: into the worship of this amazing being. This entailed two to three hours of daily meditation, *japa* (mantra repetition) during daily activities, reading every word said by or written about him, including daily readings of *The Gospel of Sri Ramakrishna*, and chanting. I continued this sadhana quite happily for ten years.

I then encountered a disciple of Sri Ramana Maharshi, Gangaji, who said 'Stop! Be still, you are already That'. The message being that the effort and search were masking that which is always present; all that was required was to 'stop' and see what is always here. After many years of struggle and effort this news came like a breath of fresh air and I glimpsed the essence, that undeniable ever-present reality. This was followed by a seven day silent retreat which resulted in my first 'Awakening', and also in an ecstasy that slowly faded over the following year.

My first book *Beyond the Separate Self, The End of Anxiety and Mental Suffering* came about from the realization that occurred then and has matured over the following 12 years. During this time I wrote a series of articles, for an e-mail news group, based on my meditations and contemplations, around which that book is based. At the same time I have also completed an honours degree in comparative religion and philosophy, using the insights gained by my spiritual practices to inform my essays. Some of these essays were adapted to include as chapters in that book.

My honours thesis, together with an essay about Ramakrishna used to highlight the themes explored, has now also been published by www.nonduality.com under the title: *Humanity, Our Place in the*

Universe, The Central Beliefs of the World's Religions. I have also continued writing articles and replying to questions which has resulted in more books. As this is written there are thirteen, including this book:

Beyond The Separate Self - The End of Anxiety and Mental Suffering 2009

A Light Unto Your Self - Self Discovery Through Investigation of Experience 2011

Awakening and Beyond - Self Recognition and its Consequences 2012

Awareness of Awareness - The Open Way 2013

The Happiness That Needs Nothing - Pointers to That Which is Always Here 2014

Freedom From Anxiety and Needless Suffering – Pointers and Practices to Aid Awakening 2015

The first five are also available in poetry form, one poem per chapter, entitled 'Poetry From *Book Title Name*'. Plus the aforementioned book comparing the world's major religions and how they define Humanity's essence and 'place' in the universe:

Humanity - Our Place in the Universe - The Central Belief's of the World's Religions 2010

So, as you can see, I always have at least two books in the pipeline, without necessarily intending to write more 'books', due to the replies, articles and poems that are being written. There is another book of poems almost completed, and I have some articles for the following one already 'squirreled' away ... The books have also been made available in all formats, hard-copy, .pdf, epub, and Kindle (.mobi) from various outlets including Amazon, Nook, Ibookstore and many other book stores around the world. Also all of my articles and poems are distributed freely to my email group (which all are welcome to join at colin108@dodo.com.au) normally before they are incorporated into a book.

One further point that I would like to make is that writing the books has been an absolute blessing for me as it has unfolded over the years. The recording of the discoveries, answering questions, and the honing of the texts, has been a joy and has increased and prolonged my periods of 'wakefulness'. On re-reading the manuscripts so many times, for editing and verification purposes, I have come to realize that I (the separate self) do not write them at all but that they come from, and through, this limited manifestation of Pure Awareness. As such they are bound to contain some errors due to the limitedness of the manifestation, but hopefully these will become corrected as further discoveries occur. Thus they will always be 'works in progress', which is wonderful for it will spur me: on to overcome its limitations by further investigation, contemplation and meditation. So I would absolutely encourage you, the reader, to record your own discoveries, and never be totally content with what you have written, so that your record will inspire you and encourage you to deeper investigation/contemplation/meditation.

If you wish to contact me: with any questions or feedback you may do so at colin108@dodo.com.au

Glossary

Many of the following may not have been used in this book, although they have in the preceding ones, and I have included them as you may find them useful in future reading on this subject.

Advaita: non-dual.

Anatta: no individual separate self.

Anicca: impermanence.

Atman: Brahman within each individual, that portion of The Absolute in each person.

Bodhisattva: one who seeks full enlightenment so as to aid others to do the same.

Brahman: the all-pervading transcendental Absolute Reality.

Darshan: the blessing or purification felt in the presence of holiness.

Kali: the Divine Mother, creator, preserver and destroyer. Sakti, cosmic energy, consciousness in motion.

Lila: the divine play or manifestation, consciousness in motion.

Mahayana: the 'great vehicle' capable of carrying many people to liberation, as a bodhisattva is one who vows not to enter into *parinirvana* until all creatures are liberated.

Maya: The power of Brahman, which supports the cosmic illusion of the One appearing as the many.

Nirvana: Buddhist word for *moksa*, enlightenment, Awakening.

Nitya: the Ultimate Reality, the eternal Absolute.

Parinirvana: The nirvana that a fully enlightened being enters after death, from which there is no reincarnation.

Prakriti: the manifestation, nature.

Purusa: the witnessing consciousness, or Awareness, according to Samkhya unique to each individual.

Sakti: cosmic energy, consciousness in motion.

Satchitananda: existence (*sat*), consciousness (*chit*), bliss (*ananda*).

Siva: universal consciousness when it is at rest, aware of every movement occurring in it, which is 'Pure Awareness'.

Upanishads: the last works of the Vedas, in which ritual was supplanted by the personal and mystical experiencing of The Absolute (Brahman).

Bibliography

Barks C., *The Essential Rumi,* 1995, Penguin, Harmondsworth

Drake, C., *A Light Unto Your Self,* 2011, Beyond Awakening Publications, Tomewin

Drake, C., *Awakening and Beyond,* 2012, Beyond Awakening Publications, Tomewin

Drake, C., *Awareness of Awareness,* 2013, Beyond Awakening Publications, Tomewin

Drake, C., *Beyond The Separate Self,* 2009, Beyond Awakening Publications, Tomewin

Drake, C., *Freedom From Anxiety and Needless Suffering,* 2015, Beyond Awakening Publications, Tomewin

Drake, C., *Humanity - Our Place in The Universe,* 2010, Beyond Awakening Publications, Tomewin

Drake, C., *Poetry From Beyond The Separate Self,* 2012, Beyond Awakening Publications, Tomewin

Drake, C., *The Happiness That Needs Nothing,* 2014, Beyond Awakening Publications, Tomewin

Maharshi Sri, *Words of Grace,* 1969, Sri Ramanasramam, Tiruvannamalai

Nikhilananda, S., *The Gospel of Ramakrishna,* 1942, Ramakrishna Math, Chenai

Osho, *The Language of Existence,* 1988, The Rebel Publishing House, Cologne

Powell., *The Ultimate Medicine,* 1995, Motilal Banarsidass, Delhi

Prahbavananda, Sw., *The Upanishads,* 1986, Ramakrishna Math, Myalpore

Sogyal Rinpoche, *The Tibetan Book of Living and Dying,* 1992, Harper Collins, San Francisco

Talbot M., *The Holographic Universe,* 1996, Harper Collins, London

Printed in Great Britain
by Amazon